BRANCH LINES AROUND TOWCESTER

Vic Mitchell and Keith Smith

MP Middleton Press

Front cover: A transfer freight from Woodford Halse to Woodford West Junction shunts its train in front of the ex-GCR signal box on the ex-S&MJR line at Woodford West on 9th March 1957. The spur from Woodford Halse over which the train has arrived is on the left. The loco is class L1 2-6-4T no. 67789. (N.Sprinks)

Back cover: Banbury Merton Street is seen after withdrawal of the Towcester service. Two railcars are attached to one another, this necessitating provision of two sets of wooden steps. The date is 4th July 1959 and gas lighting continued. (J.Langford)

Published November 2008

ISBN 978 1 906008 39 0

© Middleton Press, 2008

Design Deborah Esher
Typesetting Barbara Mitchell

Published by
  Middleton Press
  Easebourne Lane
  Midhurst
  West Sussex
  GU29 9AZ
Tel: 01730 813169
Fax: 01730 812601
Email: info@middletonpress.co.uk
www.middletonpress.co.uk

Printed & bound by Biddles Ltd, Kings Lynn

CONTENTS

INDEX

ACKNOWLEDGEMENTS

We are very grateful for the assistance received from many of those mentioned in the credits also to B.Bennett, W.R.Burton, A.R.Carder, L.Crosier, M.Dart, G.Croughton, F.Hornby, S.C.Jenkins, D.K.Jones, N.Langridge, B.Lewis, D.Mitchell, Mr D. and Dr S. Salter, T.Walsh, E.Wilmshurst and in particular, our always supportive wives, Barbara Mitchell and Janet Smith.

I. The S&MJ section of the LMS is shown with a solid line. The two
stations east of Towcester were short lived. (Railway Magazine)

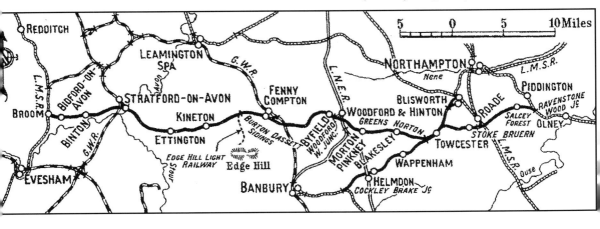

GEOGRAPHICAL SETTING

Most of the lines are on clays of different types, notably Middle and Lower Lias. The ironstone content of these, although rather low, gave rise to substantial rail traffic during the life of the system. There is also Limestone near Blisworth. Agriculture and forestry generated another substantial proportion of revenue.

The undulating landform is reflected in the gradient profiles, which are shown at the start of each section and were issued in 1916.

The most notable waterway is the River Avon which flows south under the line at Stratford and then west, close to it for six miles or so. The suffix for this town has *on* or *upon*, with or without hyphens, and consistency is impossible, except in the titles of our albums. The pronunciation of Towcester is worthy of note: it is most commonly "*Toaster*".

The other well known river is the Ouse, which is close to where we start our journey, in the east at Olney.

The maps are to the scale of 25ins to 1 mile, with north at the top, unless otherwise indicated.

HISTORICAL BACKGROUND

To set the scene, we will look at the south-north lines with which our east-west route was associated. It branched off the Midland Railway's 1872 Bedford-Northampton line near Olney at Ravenstone Wood Junction, passed over the London & Birmingham Railway of 1838 (London & North Western Railway from 1846) near Roade, ran above the 1898 Great Central Railway south of Woodford, bridged over the 1852 Great Western Railway south of Fenny Compton and linked with the same company at Stratford upon Avon. This was the 1859/60 route between Hatton and Honeybourne. The western junction was at Broom, on the 1866 Evesham & Redditch Railway, which became part of the MR in 1882.

The East & West Junction Railway was empowered on 23rd June 1864 to build a line from the Northampton & Banbury Junction Railway at Greens Norton Junction to Stratford. This opened on 1st June 1871 between Fenny Compton and Kineton, with the sections both sides following, on 1st July 1873.

The route westwards was authorised on 5th August 1873 and was opened by the Evesham, Redditch & Stratford upon Avon Railway on 2nd June 1879.

Banbury had received its first railway when the Buckinghamshire Railway was completed from Bletchley in 1850, the northern terminus opening on 1st May. This line was linked to Towcester on 1st June 1872 by the N&BJR. Its first section, from Blisworth, had opened to Towcester in June 1866, but it never served Northampton. It was known optimistically as the "Midland Counties & South Wales Railway" initially and was just 4¼ miles long. The assumed name and poor financial condition resulted in it becoming a local joke.

Due to financial problems, the E&WJR was closed to passengers from 1st August 1877 until 2nd March 1885. Despite this, the company promoted an Act, which was passed on 15th August 1879, to enable its trains to run between Bedford, Roade and Towcester. It was named the Easton Neston Mineral, & Towcester, Roade & Olney Junction Railway, but in 1882 the name was changed to the Stratford-upon-Avon, Towcester & Midland Junction Railway. The section between Towcester and Olney did not open until 13th April 1891, and then for freight only. A passenger service ran briefly, between 1st December 1892 and 31st March 1893.

The three lines were financial disasters and eventually came together under the control of a new company, the Stratford-upon-Avon & Midland Junction Railway, on 1st January 1909. This took over the N&BJR on 29th April 1910, giving it links to Blisworth and Banbury.

The SMJR lasted until the Grouping, when it became part of the London Midland & Scottish Railway on 1st January 1923. This competed with the GWR for the London-Bristol freight traffic from 1927, by using this east-west route. Much upgrading took place and this proved to be of great value during World War II. The route became part of the London Midland Region of British Railways upon nationalisation in 1948.

Passenger service withdrawals were as follows, with approximate freight route closures in brackets: Stratford to Broom - 16th June 1947 (1960), Blisworth to Banbury - 2nd July 1951 (south end 1953) and Blisworth to Stratford - 7th April 1952 (1964). Freight ran east of Towcester until 22nd June 1958, when the line was severed by the M1; detailed dates are given in the captions. The Fenny Compton-Kineton section was retained for access to a military depot. The line west of Fenny Compton had been transferred to the Western Region on 1st February 1958. It was leased to the Ministry of Defence from 18th July 1971 and Railtrack was responsible for it from 1st January 2001.

PASSENGER SERVICES

It seems that all trains ran on weekdays only.

Olney to Towcester
This brief timetable is shown near picture no. 8.

Blisworth to Banbury
The initial service between Blisworth and Towcester was of six trains. After operation was extended to Banbury, there were generally four, but this had been reduced to two by 1887.

The service had recovered to four by 1910, but was cut back to three in 1915. Wartime economies brought a reduction to two in 1917 and it remained at this low level until the end in 1951.

For many years there was an extra train on Thursdays for marketgoers, but not in the later years.

Blisworth to Broom Junction
There were six trains on the initial service between Fenny Compton and Kineton, with six on offer for the extended operation to Stratford. This diminished to two in the period prior to the prolonged closure.

Upon reopening, five trains were on offer. The figures varied east and west of Stratford. For example in 1909 they were 6 and 4, while in 1933 they were 3 and 4. By this time, there were one or two through coaches from Euston to Stratford upon Avon. There was also one from Marylebone via Woodford until February 1936. The Woodford-Stratford local service began in 1899 and usually comprised two trains, but latterly only one. There had earlier been some short workings between Woodford and Byfield to provide connections with the GCR.

August 1871

EAST and WEST JUNCTION	[Sec., C. Banks.							
Down.		Week Days.						No Sunday Trains.
	1&2	1,2,3	1&2	1,2,3	1,2,3	1&2	1&2	
Fenny Compton..dep	7 45	9 0	10 21	1 18	2 46	5 33	8 18	
Kineton ....arr	8 10	9 25	10 45	1 43	3 5	5 58	8 40	
Up.	1&2	1&2	1&2	1,2,3	1,2,3	1&2	1&2	
Kineton ....dep	7 5	8 30	9 45	12 40	2 10	4 55	7 5	
Fenny Comptn 21,18	7 30	8 55	10 8	1 5	2 35	5 20	7 30	

December 1873

BLISWORTH, TOWCESTER, FENNY COMPTON and STRATFORD-ON-AVON.—
Gen. Man., James R. Burke.]   East and West Junction   [Sec., C. Banks.

	mrn	mrn	non	aft		aft	aft	&c. frm	Up.	mrn	mrn	aftn	mrn	aftn	aft	aft
Euston Sta. LONDON 120		3 0	9 0	2 0		3 0	6 0	Stratfo d	23 WORCESTER dep			7 0		10 0	12 3	3 0
NRTHMPTN ,,	8 10	10 55	1 10		4 15	7 18	cl	2 cl. 3 cl	Strtford.-on-A.	6 20	8 3	8 55		11 4	2 50	5 1
Blisworth dep	9 10	11 0	1 50		5 0	7 55	2	8 0 5	Ettington	6 34	8 45	9 1		13 12	2 36	3 25
Towcester ,,	9 21	11 12	2 1	2 2	5 12	7 2	cl	2	Kineton [19, 16	6 45	9 0	9 22		121 2	6 6	6 35
Blakesley ...	9 32	1126	13	2 25	5 28	8 24	2	3 4	FennyCrompton	7	9 20	9 6	10 14	23 3	2 3	4 3
Morta Pinkny	9 40	1135	2 2	2 35	5 37	8 33 4	8 2	10 10	Byfield ..	7 16		9 54	1 1	12 46	3 19	7 3
Byfield[16,19	9 51	1146	2 3	1 19	5 49	8 44 5	7 3	2	Mort n Pinkney	7 27		14	1113	257	3 30	7 13
Fenny Cmptn	10 7	12 2	3 2	1 26	1 9	10 4	8 4	2 6	Blakesley ..127	7 32		1017	1154	1 6	3 39	7 3
Kineton....	1091	12 4	3 14	4 40	6 35	9 14	7 1 4	3 2 10	Tow's er 127 arr	7 49		1035	1210	20 3	5 55	7 32
Ettington [15	1032	1237	3 27	4 52	6 46	9 25 8	0 5	0 3 2 4	Blisworth 125	7 59		104 3	1240	3 4	5 7	42
Strtfrd-on-A.	1045	1240	3 40	5 10	7 1	9 40 8	8 5	4 3 6 4	NRTHMPTN arr	9 25		1190	1257	1 55	4 30	7 55
22 WOR STR ar	1212		6 0			9 0	13 6	8 5	LONDON 125..	9 40		1250		4 0	6 5	1030

NORTHAMPTON and BANBURY JUNCTION.

Traff. Supt., George Porter, Blisworth: Sec. and Gen. Man., J. W. Theobald, 148, Gresham House, Old Broad Street, E. C.

Miles from Blisworth.	Fares from Blisworth. 1 cl. s. d.	2 cl. s. d.	3 cl. s. d.	gov s. d.	*Fm M'rkt Harbro, p. 133*	mrn	mrn	aft	aft	
					120 LONDON (Euston) dp	6 15	11 0	3 0	6 0	....
					124 L'POOL (Lime St.) ,,	4 0	7 10	1140	1 0	....
					PETERBRO' 133 ,,	6 15	8 40	2 20	5 30	....
					133 NORTHAMPTN a ,,	8 10	1020	4 15	7 18	....
					Blisworth (N. & B. J.) dp	8 40	1250	4 45	7 45	....
4¼	1 0	0 8	0 6	0 4	Towcester	8 50	1 5	5 5	7 55	....
8¼	2 0	1 4	1 0	0 8	Wappenham	9 0	1 15	5 15	8 5	....
12	3 0	2 0	1 6	0 11½	Helmdon	9 8	1 25	5 25	8 15	....
16¾	4 0	2 8	2 0	1 4	Farthinghoe c 132	9 22	1 35	5 45	8 30	....
20¾	5 0	3 4	2 6	1 8	**Banbury 16, 19** arr	9 34	1 47	6 0	8 42	....

Mls	*Fm Leamington, p. 19.*	mrn	mrn	aft	aft		
—	**Banbury** (Melton Rd) dp	7 14	10 5	2 20	6 30	....	....
4	Farthinghoe d	7 21	1012	2 30	6 37	....	....
8¾	Helmdon	7 36	1027	2 48	6 52	....	....
12½	Wappenham	7 44	1035	2 50	7 2	....	....
16¼	Towcester 133 [133	7 51	1045	3 20	7 12	....	....
20¾	**Blisworth 120, 125,** a	8 4	1055	3 30	7 25	....	....
25¼	133 NORTHAMPTN a arr	8b53	113[illegible]	3 55	7 55	....	....
68	PETERBRO' 133 ,,	1115	1 55	6 25	9 45	....	....
159½	121 L'POOL (Lime St.) ,,	1 0	4 15	7 45	....	....	....
83¾	125 LONDON (Euston) ,,	9 40	1250	6 5	1030	....	....

b Castle Station.

a Bridge Street Station. c Stop to set down only. d Stop to take up only.

Decen
1873

BLISWORTH, TOWCESTER, and BANBURY.—Northampton and Banbury Junction.

Traff. Supt., E. Stanton. Sec., John Crick.

Miles frm Blisworth	*Fm. Markt Harbro', p. 189*	gov	mrn		aft	aft	
	170 LONDON (Euston) dep	7 15	1010		3 0	6 0	....
	174 L'POOL (Lime St.) ,,	2b35	9 45		12b0	4 5	....
	NRTHMPTN (Cstle) ,,	8 50	1250		4 20	7 52	....
	Blisworth (N. & B. J.) dep	9 11	1 10	Thursdays	4 41	8 5	....
4¼	Towcester	9 28	1 25		4 56	8 20	....
8¼	Wappenham	9 42	1 40		5 9	....	....
12	Helmdon	9 52	1 52		5 21	....	....
16¾	Farthinghoe c 191	10 8	2 5		5 37	....	....
20¾	Banbury 20, 23 arr	1018	2 15		5 45	....	....

Mls	*From Leamington, p. 23.*	gov	mrn	aft		aft
—	**Banbury** (Melton Rd.) dp	7 40	1045	3 18	Thursdays	6 5
4	Farthinghoe a	7 47	1052	3 25		6 12
8¾	Helmdon	8 2	11 7	3 41		6 27
12½	Wappenham	8 14	1119	3 54		6 39
16½	Towcester 168 [and below	8 30	1135	4 10		6 52
20¾	**Blisworth 170, 175,** arr	8 45	1150	4 25		7 7
25½	NRTHMPTN. (Cstle) arr	9 14	12 5	4 50		7 25
159½	171 L'POOL (Lime St.) ,,	1 50	4b50	8 30		....
83¾	175 LONDON (Euston) ,,	1030	2 30	7b25	b	1015

a Stops to take up only. b *Via* Northampton (Castle Station). c Stops to set down.

February 188

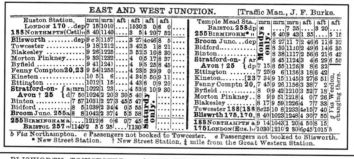

EAST AND WEST JUNCTION.

[Traffic Man., J. F. Burke.

Euston Station,		mrn	mrn	aft	aft	aft	aft	
LONDON 170 ..dep		7 15	1010	....	1b30	3 0	6 0	....
188 NORTHMPTN (Cstl) ,,		8 40	1140	....	3 5	4 20	7 52	....
Blisworth ....dep		9c3	1157	....	3 27	4c46	8 5	....
Towcester		9 18	1212	....	3 42	5 1	8 21	....
Blakesley		9 26	1225	....	3 52	5 10	8 30	....
Morton Pinkney		9 33	1232	....	4 0	5 17	8 37	....
Byfield		9 41	1241	....	4 9	5 25	8 45	....
Fenny Compton 20, 23		9 54	1255	....	4 23	5 39	9 0	....
Kineton		10 5	1 6	....	4 34	5 50	9 11	....
Ettington		1012	1 15	....	4 43	6 0	9 20	....
Stratford-on-Avon † 25 a	mrn	1022	1 23	....	4 53	6 10	9 30	....
d	7 50	1024	2 20	3 30	5 40	Saturdy only.	....	....
Binton	7 57	1031	2 27	3 45	5 47		....	....
Bidford	8 5	1039	2 34	4 0	5 55		....	....
Broom Junc. 255 a	8 8	1042	2 37	4 5	5 58		....	....
255 BIRMINGHAM a	....	1212	6 0	6 0	7 45		....	....
BRISTOL 257 ,,	1140	2 5	5 25	....	1130		....	....

Temple Mead Sta.,	mrn	mrn	mrn	aft	aft	aft
BRISTOL 258 dp	Mondys only.	....	7 35	....	3 20	....
255 BIRMINGHM* ,,		6 40	9 43	1 35	....	5 15
Broom Junc. ...dep		8 27	11 7	2 46	6 11	6 32
Bidford		8 30	1110	2 49	6 14	6 35
Binton		8 38	1117	2 56	6 21	6 42
Stratford-on-Avon † 25 ar		8 45	1124	3 4	6 29	6 50
dp	7 15	8 55	1126	3 8	6 32	*g Via* Weedon, changing there.
Ettington	7 25	9 6	1136	3 18	6 42	
Kineton ......[23	7 34	9 15	1145	3 27	6 51	
Fenny Comptn 20,	7 45	9 26	1156	3 38	7 2	
Byfield	8 0	9 42	1210	3 52	7 18	
Morton Pinkney	8 9	9 51	1218	4 0	7 26	
Blakesley	8 17	9 59	1226	4 7	7 33	
Towcester 188 [188	8e25	10 8	1233	4e15	7 40	
Bliswrth 175, 170,	8 40	1023	1248	4 30	7 55	
188 NORTHAMPTN a	9 14	1043	1 20	4 50	8 15	
175 LONDON (Eus.) ,,	1030	1210	2 30	6g45	1015	b

b *Via* Northampton. c Passengers not booked to Towcester. e Passengers not booked to Blisworth.
* New Street Station. † New Street Station, ¼ mile from the Great Western Station.

February 1887

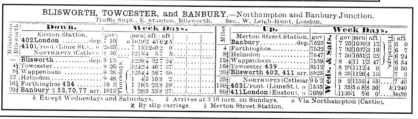

BLISWORTH, TOWCESTER, and BANBURY.—Northampton and Banbury Junction.

Traffic Supt., E. Stanton, Blisworth. Sec., W. Leigh-Hunt, London.

Miles from Blisworth	**Down.** Euston Station,	Week Days. gov		mrn	aft	aft			
	402 London ....dep.	7 10		o 1010	2 45	6z5	....	....	....
	410 L'POOL (Lime St.) .. ,,	2b35	....	7 15	12b0	2 0	....	....	....
	NORTHMPTN (Cstle) ,,	8 50	....	1215	4 5	7 5	....	....	....
—	**Blisworth** ....dep.	9 13	Thursdays.	1230	4 32	7 24	....	....	....
4¼	Towcester	9 26		1242	4 46	7 37	....	....	....
8¼	Wappenham	9 38		1254	4 58	7 50	....	....	....
12	Helmdon	9 48		1 4	5 10	8 2	....	....	....
16¾	Farthinghoe 434	10 3		1 19	5 23	8 19	....	....	....
20¾	**Banbury** ‖ 53, 70, 77 arr.	1013		1 28	5 33	8 27	....	....	....

Miles	**Up.** Merton Street Station,	Week Days. gov		gov	mrn	aft		aft
	Banbury ....dep.	7b25	Weds. & Sats.	7 25	1030	3 12	Thursdays.	6 0
4	Farthinghoe	7b32		7 32	1037	3 19		6 7
8¾	Helmdon	7b47		7 50	1051	3 35		6 24
12½	Wappenham	7b59		8 4	11 1	3 47		6 34
16½	Towcester 439	8b12		8 20	1112	4 0		6 50
20¾	**Blisworth 402, 411** arr.	8b25		8 35	1126	4 13		7 3
25¼	NORTHMPTN (Cstle) ar	9b2		9 2	1155	4 55	....	7 40
150¼	403 L'POOL (Lime St.) ,,	1b35		1 35	5o8	8 50	k	1240
80¾	411 London (Euston) ,,	10b9		1130	1 5	6 0	....	9o50

b Except Wednesdays and Saturdays. k Arrives at 3 10 mrn. on Sundays. o Via Northampton (Castle).
z By slip carriage. ‖ Merton Street Station.

July 1908

July 1910

BLISWORTH, TOWCESTER, BANBURY, WOODFORD, STRATFORD-ON-AVON, & BROOM JUNCTION.—(1st and 3rd class).—

Stratford-upon-Avon and Midland Junction.

Offices—Stratford-on-Avon. Traff. Man. and Eng., Russell Willmott. Sec. and Acct., A. E. Diggins.

Miles from Blisworth.	**Down.** Euston Station,	mrn	mrn	mrn	mrn	mrn	mrn	mrn	aft	aft	aft	aft	aft
	404 London ....dep.	....	....	7 10	....	9g20	10c9	10c9	p	2l45	....	4c30	6g5
	404 BLETCHLEY .... ,,	....	....	8 12	....	10 0	11½c	11½c	....	4 5	r	4c44	6 50
	412 MANCHESTER §.. ,,	....	c	1155	....	....	8 30	8 30	....	1150	c	2 10	2c10
	413 RUGBY .... ,,	....	....	8 30	....	9 40	1110	1110	....	3c8	....	5c15	5c35
	NORTHAMPTN (C.) ,,	....	....	8 50	....	1030	1215	1 5	....	4 23	....	6 0	7 5
—	**Blisworth** ....dep.	....	....	9 10	9 20	1045	1238	1 22	....	4 45	....	6 15	7 27
4¼	Towcester ....arr.	....	....	9 18	9 28	1053	1246	1 30	....	4 53	....	6 25	7 35
—	Towcester ....dep.	....	....	....	9 30	....	1247	....	....	4 54	....	....	7 36
8¼	Wappenham	....	....	....	9 39	....	1255	....	....	5 2	....	....	7 44
12	Helmdon	....	....	....	9 47	....	1 2	....	....	5 9	....	....	7 51
16¾	Farthinghoe 440	....	....	....	9 58	....	1 13	....	....	5 20	....	....	8 2
20¾	**Banbury** ‖ 74, 81 arr.	....	....	....	10 5	....	1 20	....	....	5 27	....	....	8 9
—	Towcester ....dep.	....	....	9 19	....	....		1 32	....	Stop	....	6 26	....
8½	Blakesley	....	....	9 28	....	....		1 41	....	....	....	6 35	....
11¾	Morton Pinkney	....	....	9 35	....	....		1 48	....	....	....	6 42	....
15¾	Byfield ....arr.	....	....	9 42	....	....		1 55	....	....	....	6 49	....
—	Byfield ....dep.	....	....	9 46	....	....		2 8	....	....	....	6 53	....
17¾	**Woodford * 636**..arr.	....	....	9 50	....	....		2 12	....	aft	....	6 57	....
—	636 London (M'lebone) d	....	....	6 50	....	10h0	Thursdays only.	1215	....	4h30		6b20	....
—	636 AYLESBURY ...... ,,	....	....	8 6	....	9 40		1219	....	4 59		6 18	....
—	642 SHEFFIELD (Vic.).. ,,	....	5 35	5 35	....	8 50		1121	....	3 27		4 55	....
—	643 LEICESTER (Cen.).. ,,	....	8 14	8 14	....	1010		1250	....	4 49		6 23	....
—	643 RUGBY (Central).. ,,	....	8 38	8 38	....	9 38		1 15	....	4 24		6 51	....
—	**Woodford ***.......dep.	....	9 10	9 24	....	1135		1 58	....	6 7	Saturdays only.	7 45	....
—	Byfield ....arr.	....	9 14	9 28	....	1139		2 2	....	6 11		7 49	....
—	Byfield ....dep.	....	....	9 46	....	1140		2 7	....	6 13		7 50	....
22¾	Fenny Compton 74, 81.	....	....	9 58	....	1151	Stop	2 18	....	6 24		8 1	....
29	Kineton	....	....	1012	....	12 2		2 29	....	6 35		8 12	....
33	Ettington	....	....	1020	....	1210	....	2 37	....	6 43		8 20	....
38½	**Stratford-on-Avon † 96, 97** arr.	....	....	1029	....	1219	aft	2 40	....	6 52		8 29	....
	dep.	7 40	....	1031	....	....	2 0	....	5 40	....	8 7	....	....
42	Binton	7 48	....	1039	....	....	2 8	....	5 48	....	8 15	....	....
44½	Bidford-on-Avon	7 56	....	1047	....	....	2 16	....	5 56	....	8 23	....	....
45½	**Broom** Junc. 571..arr.	8 0	....	1051	....	....	2 20	....	6 0	....	8 27	....	....
56	571 REDDITCH ......arr.	8 32	....	1128	....	....	3 3	....	6 44	....	9 2	....	....
52½	571 EVESHAM ...... ,,	8 28	....	1118	....	....	2 51	....	6 28	....	8 53	....	....
70¾	573 CHELTENHAM ‡. ,,	9 25	....	1213	....	....	4 8	....	7 56	....	....	....	....

Miles.	**Up.**	mrn	mrn	mrn	mrn	mrn	mrn	mrn	aft	aft	aft	aft	aft	aft
	578 CHELTENHAM ‡ ..dep.	....	....	....	....	....	....	9 22	1 27	....	....	....	4 45	....
	571 EVESHAM ...... ,,	....	....	7 52	....	....	....	10 42	2 18	....	....	....	5 55	8 15
	571 REDDITCH ...... ,,	....	....	7 42	....	....	....	10 34	2 2	....	....	....	5 44	8 14
—	**Broom** Junction....dep.	....	....	8 16	....	....	....	11 10	2 42	....	Runs on the 5th, 11th, 19th, and 25th instant.	From Blisworth.	6 20	8 42
1¼	Bidford-on-Avon	....	....	8 21	....	....	....	11 15	2 47	....			6 25	8 47
2¾	Binton	....	....	8 29	....	....	....	11 23	2 55	....			6 33	8 55
7¾	**Stratford-on-Avon † 96, 97** arr.	....	....	8 36	....	....	....	11 30	3 2	....			6 40	9 2
	dep.	....	8a0	Stop	9 55	....	....	12 20	Stop	4 35			7 30	Saturdays only.
12¾	Ettington	....	8 12		10 5	....	....	12 32		4 45			7 41	
16¾	Kineton	....	8 21	....	1012	....	....	12 40	....	4 52			7 49	
23¼	Fenny Compton 74, 81.	....	8 33	....	1023	....	....	12 51	....	5 3			8 1	
30	Byfield ....arr.	....	8 44	mrn	1034	....	....	1 2	aft	5 14			8 12	
—	Byfield ....dep.	....	8 48	9 46	1035	....	....	1 8	2 8	5 15		6 53	8 17	
32	**Woodford *643**..arr	....	8 52	9 50	1039	....	....	1 12	2 12	5 19		6 57	8 21	
46¼	636 RUGBY (Central) arr.	....	9 47	1018	1147		....	2 10	4 5	6 4		7 23	9 24	
66	636 LEICESTER (Cen.) ,,	....	1022	1044	12 9		....	2 32	4 28	6 29		7 48	9 59	
127¾	637 SHEFFIELD (Vic.) ,,	....	1228	1228	1 32		....	4 1	5 56	8 8		9 36	1n55	
63	643 AYLESBURY .... ,,	....	9 37	1054	....			2 9	3 27	....		7 45	....	
101	643 London (M'lebone) ,,	....	1025	1155	12 5			3 0	4 44	6 43		8 39	9 55	
—	**Woodford ***......dep.	....	9 24	....	....	Thursdays only.	Wednesdays and Saturdays.	11 35	Stop	....		Stop	7 45	....
—	Byfield ....arr.	....	9 28	....	....			11 39		....			7 49	....
—	Byfield ....dep.	....	9 37	....	....			1 4	....	....	5 19	....	8 14	....
34¼	Morton Pinkney	....	9 47	....	....			1 12	....	....	5 29	....	8 22	....
37¼	Blakesley	....	9 53	....	....			1 18	....	....	5 35	....	8 29	....
41¼	Towcester ....arr.	....	10 0	....	....			1 25	aft	....	5 42	aft	8 36	....
—	Mls **Banbury** ‖ ....dep.	7 25	....	....	....	1040		12k45	3d35	....	....	5 47	....	....
—	4 Farthinghoe	7 33	....	....	....	1047		12k52	3d43	....	....	5 54	....	....
—	8¾ Helmdon	7 47	....	....	....	1057		1k2	3d54	....	....	6 6	....	....
—	12¾ Wappenham	7 58	....	....	....	11 4		1k9	4d3	....	....	6 14	....	....
—	16¾ Towcester.....arr.	8 7	....	....	....	1111		1k16	4d12	....	....	6 21	....	....
—	Towcester ....dep.	8 10	10 1	....	....	1115	1115	1 30	4 15	....	5 45	6 50	8 38	....
45¾	**Blisworth 404, 413** arr.	8 20	1011	....	....	1125	1125	1 40	4 25	....	5 55	7 0	8 48	....
50¼	NORTHAMPTON (C.) ar	9 3	1030	....	....	1155	1155	1 58	5 0	....	6 8	7 45	9 10	....
65½	404 RUGBY .... ,,	9 20	1115	....	....	1q50	1q50	2 40	5 11	....	7c39	8 0	1046c	
171½	405 MANCHESTER § .. ,,	1230	2 27	....	....	4c45	4c45	6 5	8 15	c	1038	1 10	3c0	....
62	413 BLETCHLEY ..... ,,	9 0	1052	....	....	1156	1156	2 16	6 10	....	6c45	8 30	9c52	....
108¾	413 London (Euston) ,,	1010	12 0	....	....	1 5	1 5	4 5	6 0	....	8 25	9 50	1125c	

a Through Carriage to London (Marylebone).
b By Through Slip Carriage to Stratford-on-Avon.
c Via Northampton.
d Thursdays only.
g By Slip Carriage.
h Through Carriage to Stratford-on-Avon.
k Except Thursdays.
l Leaves at 2 53 aft. on Saturdays.
n Arrives at 1 40 on Sunday mornings.
p Leaves at 10 45 mrn., via Northampton, on and after the 16th instant.
q Arrives at 12 46 aft. on and after the 16th instant.
r Leaves at 4 50, via Northampton on Saturdays.
t Tuesdays only.
* Woodford and Hinton.
† S. M. J. Station, 1 mile from G. W. Station.
‡ Queen's Road, Lansdown.
§ London Road. ‖ Merton Street.

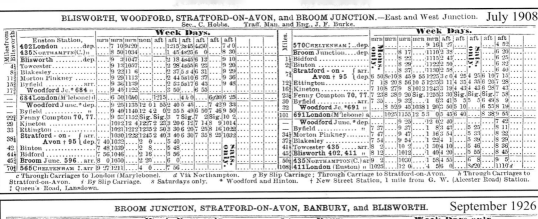

BLISWORTH, WOODFORD, STRATFORD-ON-AVON, and BROOM JUNCTION.—East and West Junction. July 1908

Sec., C. Hobbs. Traff. Man. and Eng., J. F. Burke.

Miles from Blisworth	Week Days.	mrn	mrn	mrn	non	aft	aft	aft	aft	aft	aft
	Euston Station, 402 London ....dep.	....	7 10	9i20	....	....	1215	2s45	4d30	....	7 d 0
	435 Northamptn (C.) "	....	8 50	1034	....	....	1 45	4s25	6 0	....	8 30
	Blisworth ....dep.	....	9 3	1047	....	....	2 18	4s45	6 13	....	9 10
4¼	Towcester	....	9 13	1057	....	....	2 28	4s55	6 23	....	9 20
8½	Blakesley	....	9 22	11 6	....	....	2 37	5 s 4	6 31	....	9 29
11¾	Morton Pinkney	....	9 29	1113	....	....	2 44	5s10	6 37	....	9 36
15¾	Byfield ....arr.	....	9 36	1139	....	....	2 53	5s17	6 45	....	9 48
17¾	Woodford Jc.* 684 "	....	9 45	1122	....	....	3 50	....	6 55	....	....
—	684 London (M'lebone) d	....	6 50	10h0	....	1215	....	4 h 0	....	6g20	6 25
—	Woodford Junc.* dep.	....	9 25	1135	12 0	1 55	2 40	5 45	....	7 42	9 33
—	Byfield .... "	....	9 40	1140	12 4	2 0	2 55	5 49	6 50	7 46	9 50
22¾	Fenny Compton 70, 77.	....	9 52	1152	Sig.	Sig.	3 7	Sig.	7 2	Sig.	10 2
29	Kineton	....	1012	12 4	1227	2 23	3 20	6 12	7 14	8 9	1014
33	Ettington	....	1021	1212	1235	2 30	3 30	6 20	7 25	8 16	1022
38¼	Stratford-on-Avon † 95 arr.	....	1030	1222	1245	2 40	3 40	6 30	7 35	8 25	1032
	dep.	7 40	1032	....	2 0	....	5 40	....	....	....	Sats. only.
42	Binton	7 48	1039	....	2 8	....	5 48	....	....	....	
44½	Bidford	7 56	1046	....	2 16	....	5 56	....	....	....	
45¾	Broom Junc. 596 ..arr.	8 0	1050	....	2 20	....	6 0	....	....	....	
70¾	565 Cheltenham ‡ arr	9 27	1211	....	4 0	....	7 56	....	....	....	

Miles.	Week Days.	mrn	mrn	mrn	mrn	mrn	aft	aft	aft	aft	aft
	570 Cheltenham ‡ ..dep.	Mons. only.	....	....	....	9 16	1 27	....	Sats. only.	....	4 52
	Broom Junction....dep.		....	8 17	....	1110	2 38	....		....	6 20
1¼	Bidford		....	8 22	....	1115	2 43	....		....	6 25
2¾	Binton		....	8 29	....	1122	2 50	....		....	6 32
7¾	Stratford-on-Avon † 95 arr.		....	8 37	....	1130	2 58	....		....	6 40
	dep.	6 50	8c10	8 45	9 55	1225	3 c 0	4 25	4 25	6 10	7 15
12¾	Ettington	7 1	8 20	8 56	10 5	1235	3 11	4 35	4 35	6 20	7 28
16¾	Kineton	7 10	8 27	9 8	1012	1243	3 19	4 43	4 43	6 28	7 43
23¼	Fenny Compton 70, 77.	7 23	8 38	9 20	Sig.	1255	3 30	Sig.	Sig.	Sig.	7 58
30	Byfield ....arr.	7 35	....	9 32	....	1 6	3 41	5 5	5 5	6 49	8 9
32	Woodford Jc. *691 "	....	8 52	9 45	1038	1 20	3 50	5 10	....	6 55	8 19
101	691 London (M'lebone) a	....	1025	1155	12 5	3 0	5 45	6 40	....	8 38	9 55
—	Woodford Junc. * dep.	....	....	9 25	....	12 0	2 40	....	....	....	7 42
—	Byfield .... "	7 37	....	9 37	....	1 8	3 43	....	5 25	....	8 11
34¼	Morton Pinkney	7 47	....	9 47	....	1 16	3 54	....	5 33	....	8 22
37½	Blakesley	7 54	....	9 54	....	1 22	4 1	....	5 39	....	8 29
41½	Towcester 435 .....arr.	8 2	....	10 2	....	1 30	4 10	....	5 46	....	8 36
45¾	Blisworth 402, 411 "	8 12	....	1012	....	1 40	4 20	....	5 55	....	8 45
50¼	435 Northampton (C.) ar	9 2	....	1030	....	1 58	4 55	....	6 8	....	9 5
108¾	411 London (Euston) "	1025	....	12 0	....	4 5	6 0	....	8d20	....	1110d

c Through Carriages to London (Marylebone). d Via Northampton. g By Slip Carriage; Through Carriage to Stratford-on-Avon. h Through Carriages to Stratford-on-Avon. i By Slip Carriage. s Saturdays only. * Woodford and Hinton. † New Street Station, 1 mile from G. W. (Alcester Road) Station. ‡ Queen's Road, Lansdown.

BROOM JUNCTION, STRATFORD-ON-AVON, BANBURY, and BLISWORTH. September 1926

Miles from Broom Jc.	Up. Week Days only.	mrn	mrn	mrn	mrn	aft	mrn	aft	aft	aft	aft	aft	aft
	660 Gloucester ....dep.	....	....	....	....	....	8 48	....	1 23	....	....	4s27	4 27
	660 Cheltenhm Spa A "	....	....	....	....	....	9 3	....	1 50	....	....	4s45	4 45
	726 Birmingham B "	....	....	6 32	....	....	9 50	....	1b10	....	....	5 0	7 25
—	Broom Junction....dep.	....	....	8 8	....	....	1115	....	2 55	....	....	6 30	8 50
1¼	Bidford-on-Avon	....	....	8 13	....	....	1120	....	2 59	....	....	6 34	8 54
3¾	Binton	....	....	8 21	....	....	1128	....	3 7	....	....	6 42	9 2
7½	Stratford-on-Avon C 126, 129 arr.	....	....	8 29	....	....	1135	....	3 15	....	....	6 50	9 10
	dep.	....	7A55	Stop	....	....	1215	....	Stop	....	6 10	Fridays and Saturdays.	....
12¾	Ettington	....	8 9		....	....	1227	....		....	6 22		....
16¾	Kineton	....	8 20	....	....	....	1237	....	....	....	6 32		....
23	Fenny Compton 98, 103	....	8 34	....	....	....	1249	....	....	....	6 44		....
30	Byfield ....arr.	....	8 47	....	....	....	1 2	....	....	....	6 57		....
—	Byfield ....dep.	....	8 52	....	9 55	....	1 15	....	....	220	7 8		....
32	Woodford 851 D arr.	....	8 57	....	9 59	....	1 20	....	....	225	7 13		....
101	851 London (Mar.)..arr.	....	1040	....	1236	....	3 0	....	....	457	8 55		....
—	Woodford D ....dep.	....	8 37	....	....	....	1 0	....	....	....	....		....
—	Byfield ....arr.	....	8 42	....	....	....	1 5	....	....	....	....		....
—	Byfield ....dep.	....	8 57	....	....	....	1 7	....	....	....	7 2		....
34	Morton Pinkney, for Sulgrave	....	9 7	....	....	....	1 17	....	....	....	7 13		....
37½	Blakesley	....	9 20	....	....	....	1 24	....	....	....	7 24		....
41½	Towcester ....arr.	....	9 28	mrn	....	....	1 32	....	aft	....	7 32	....	....
—	Mls Banbury F ....dep.	....	....	1055	....	....	....	....	4 55	....	....	....	....
—	4 Farthinghoe	....	....	11 4	....	....	....	....	5 4	....	....	....	....
—	8¾ Helmdon G	....	....	1117	....	....	....	....	5 17	....	....	....	....
—	12¼ Wappenham	....	....	1126	....	....	....	....	5 26	....	....	....	....
—	16¼ Towcester	....	....	1135	....	....	....	....	5 34	....	....	....	....
—	Towcester ......[467 dep.	8 10	9 32	1138	....	1250	1 35	4 57	5 35	....	7 36	....	....
45¾	Blisworth 412, 423, arr.	8 20	9 42	1148	....	1 0	1 45	5 7	5 45	....	7 46	....	....
50¼	467 Northamptn (C) arr.	8 35	10 0	1215	....	1 27	2 5	5 30	6 18	....	8 13	....	....
108¾	423 London (Euston) "	10a15	12a0	1 5	....	2 20	4 15	6 20	7 55	....	1045	....	....

Miles from Blisworth.	Down. Week Days only.	mrn	mrn	mrn	mrn	mrn	non	aft	aft	aft	aft	aft
	Euston Station. 412 London ....dep.	....	6 45	....	....	9a30	12 0	....	3 a 5	4d15	7 a 0	....
	466 Northamptn (C.) "	....	8 35	8 55	....	1 0	2 10	....	4 53	6 4	8 20	....
	Blisworth ....dep.	....	8 55	9 18	....	1 20	2 38	....	5 23	6 20	8 40	....
4¼	Towcester ....arr.	....	9 4	9 27	....	1 29	2 47	....	5 32	6 29	8 49	....
—	Towcester ....dep.	....	....	9 29	....	....	....	....	5 41	....	....	....
8¼	Wappenham	....	....	9 38	....	....	....	....	5 51	....	....	....
12	Helmdon G	....	....	9 47	....	....	....	....	6 3	....	....	....
16¾	Farthinghoe ....[467	....	....	9 59	....	....	....	....	6 17	....	....	....
20¾	Banbury F 98, 103 ar	....	....	10 8	....	....	....	....	6 25	....	....	....
—	Towcester ....dep.	....	9 7	Stop	....	1 35	....	....	Stop	6 30	....	....
8½	Blakesley ....[grave	....	9 16		....	1 44	....	....		6 39	....	....
11¾	Morton Pinkney, for Sul-	....	9 24	....	....	1 53	....	....	....	6 48	....	....
15¾	Byfield ....arr.	....	9 33	....	....	2 2	....	....	....	6 57	....	....
—	Byfield ....dep.	....	9 55	....	....	2 20	....	....	....	7 8	....	....
17¾	Woodford D 844 arr.	....	9 59	....	....	2 25	....	Fridays and Saturdays.	....	7 13	....	....
—	844 London (Mar.)..dep.	....	6 45	....	10 0	1215	....		....	....	....	6T20
—	Woodford D ....dep.	8 37	9 20	....	1 0	2 7	....		....	....	....	7 47
—	Byfield ....arr.	8 42	9 25	....	1 5	2 12	....		....	....	....	7 52
—	Byfield ....dep.	Stop	9 38	....	....	2 18	....		....	....	....	7 54
22¾	Fenny Compton 98, 103		9 52	....	....	2 32	....		....	....	....	8 7
29	Kineton	....	10 5	....	....	2 45	....		....	....	....	8 20
33	Ettington	....	1015	....	....	2 55	....		....	....	....	8 30
38¼	Stratford-on-Avon C 126, 129 arr.	mrn	1025	aft	....	3 5	....		aft	....	....	8 40
	dep.	7 20	1030	2 15	....	....	....	5 55	7 40	....	....	....
42	Binton	7 31	1040	2 24	....	....	....	6 4	7 49	....	....	....
44½	Bidford-on-Avon	7 41	1049	2 33	....	....	....	6 12	7 57	....	....	....
45¾	Broom Junc. 726 ..arr.	7 45	1052	2 36	....	....	....	6 15	8 0	....	....	....
71¼	726 Birmingham B arr.	9 5	1228	4 5	....	....	....	9s4	9 43	....	....	....
70½	656 Cheltenhm Spa A "	1118	2 14	4 41	....	....	....	7 31	....	....	....	....
77¼	656 Gloucester .... "	1135	2d47	5 0	....	....	....	7 50	....	....	....	....

A Lansdown.
A Through Carriage, Stratford-on-Avon to London (Marylebone).
a Via Northampton.
B New Street.
b Departs at 1 18 aft. on Saturdays.
C 1 mile from G. W. Station.
D Woodford and Hinton (L. & N. E.)
d Arrives at 2 30 aft. on Saturdays.
F Merton Street.
G Over ¼ mile to L. & N. E. Station.
s Saturdays only.
T Through Carriage, London (Marylebone) to Stratford-on-Avon, by Slip Carriage.

BROOM JUNCTION, STRATFORD-ON-AVON, BANBURY, & BLISWORTH.—(Third class only). February 1946

Miles from Broom Jc.	Up. Week Days only	mrn	mrn	mrn	aft	aft	aft	aft
	660 Gloucester 726 dep.	..	..	..	..	..	..	..
	660 Cheltenhm A 726 "	..	..	..	..	..	..	..
	726 Birmingham B "	..	6 25	..	..	..	..	..
—	Broom Junction....dep.	..	8 15	..		..	..	..
1¼	Bidford-on-Avon	..	8 22	..		..	..	..
3¾	Binton	..	8 31	..		..	..	..
7½	Stratford-on-Avon 130, 134 arr.	..	8 42	..	Except Saturdays	..	..	..
	dep.	8 15	..	..		4S30	6 20	9 45
12¾	Ettington	8 28	..	..		4S43	6 33	9 58
16¾	Kineton	8 36	..	..		4S50	6 41	10 5
23	Fenny Compton 98, 103	8 53	..	..		Stop	6 57	Saturdays only.
30	Byfield ....arr.	9 5	..	..			7 10	
—	Byfield ....dep.	..	..	..		..	7 18	
32	Woodford C 837 arr.	..	..	..		..	7 23	
101	837 London (Mar.)..arr.	..	..	..	..	..	9 42	
—	Woodford C ....dep.	..	..	..	..	..	..	
—	Byfield ....arr.	..	..	..	..	..	..	
—	Byfield ....dep.	9 6	..	..	4 45	..	7 10	
34	Morton Pinkney, for Sul-	9 18	..	..	4 55	..	7 22	
37½	Blakesley ....[grave	9 28	..	..	5 1	..	7 29	
41½	Towcester ....arr.	9 37	..	..	5 9	aft	7 36	
—	Mls Banbury H ....dep.	..	..	1040	..	4 50	..	..
—	4 Farthinghoe	..	..	1049	..	4 59	..	..
—	8¾ Helmdon	..	..	11 2	..	5 12	..	..
—	12¼ Wappenham	..	..	1111	..	5 21	..	..
—	16¼ Towcester ......arr.	..	..	1120	..	5 30	..	..
—	Towcester ......[471 dep.	9 33	..	1121	5 10	5 31	7 37	..
45¾	Blisworth 412, 425, arr.	9 51	..	1130	5 20	5 41	7 47	..
50¼	471 Northamptn (C.) arr.	1025	..	1158	..	6 5	8 9	..
108¾	425 London (Euston) "	1240	..	1 2	..	7J50	11J30	..

Miles from Blisworth	Down. Week Days only	mrn	mrn	mrn		aft	aft	aft	aft
	Euston Station, 412 London ....dep.	..	6 45	..	..	12J15	4 30	..	..
	471 Northamptn (C.) "	..	8 29	9 0	..	2 40	5 35	6 13	..
	Blisworth ....dep.	..	8 45	9 31	..	4 0	6 0	6 36	..
4¼	Towcester ....arr.	..	8 58	9 40	..	4 10	6 8	6 44	..
—	Towcester ....dep.	..	..	9 42	..	..	6 10	..	..
8¼	Wappenham	..	..	9 51	..	..	6 22	..	..
12	Helmdon	..	..	10 0	..	..	6 32	..	..
16¾	Farthinghoe ......[468	..	..	1012	..	..	6 47	..	..
20¾	Banbury H 98, 103, arr	..	..	1020	..	..	6 55	..	..
—	Towcester ....dep.	..	9 0	..	..	4 15	Stop	6 46	..
8½	Blakesley ....[grave	..	9 10	..	..	4 23		6 54	..
11¾	Morton Pinkney, for Sul-	..	9 20	..	..	4 30	..	7 1	..
15¾	Byfield ....arr.	..	9 33	..	..	4 39	..	7 9	..
—	Byfield ....dep.	..	..	..	..		..	7 18	..
17¾	Woodford C 830 arr.	..	..	..	..		..	7 23	..
—	830 London (Mar.)..dep.	..	..	..	..		..	..	4 54
—	Woodford C ....dep.	..	..	..	..	Except Saturdays	..	..	8 25
—	Byfield ....arr.	..	..	..	..		..	..	8 30
—	Byfield ....dep.	..	9 35	..	..		..	..	8 39
22¾	Fenny Compton 98, 103	..	9 48	..	..		aft	..	8 50
29	Kineton	..	10 5	..	..		5 S0	..	9 8
33	Ettington	..	1014	..	..		5 S8	..	9 16
38¼	Stratford-on-Avon 130, 134 arr.	..	1025	..	..		5S20	..	9 27
	dep.	7 15	1030	..	..		..	..	..
42	Binton	7 27	1038	..	..	..	..	..	..
44½	Bidford-on-Avon	..	1045	..	..	..	..	..	..
45¾	Broom Junc. 726 ...arr.	7 42	1049	..	..	..	..	..	..
71¼	726 Birmingham B arr.	9 22	1226	..	..	..	..	..	..
70½	656 Cheltenhm A 726 "	9 22	5 39	..	..	..	..	..	..
77¼	656 Gloucester 726 "	9 44	6 2	..	..	..	..	..	..

A Cheltenham Spa, Lansdown. B New Street. C Woodford and Hinton (L. & N. E.). H Merton Street. J Via Northampton. S Saturdays only.

STRATFORD-ON-AVON, BANBURY, and BLISWORTH (Third class only) March 1951

Miles	Week Days only	a.m	a.m	a.m		p.m	p.m	p.m.	
	Stratford-on-Avon dep	7 12	..	1043	..	Except Sats.	..	6 40	..
6½	Ettington	7 25	..	1056	..		..	6 53	..
9½	Kineton	7 33	..	11 4	..		..	7 1	..
15½	Fenny Compton	7 47	..	1118	..		..	7 13	..
22½	Byfield A	8 0	..	1131	..	4 45	..	7 26	..
26¾	Morton Pinkney, for Sul-	8 9	..	1141	..	4 55	..	7 37	..
29¾	Blakesley ....[grave	8 16	..	1148	..	5 1	..	7 44	..
34	Towcester ....arr	8 24	..	1155	..	5 9	..	7 51	..
—	Mls Banbury D ....dep	..	1040	Sats. only	..	..	4 45	..	..
—	3¾ Farthinghoe	..	1049		..	..	4 54	..	..
—	8½ Helmdon	..	11 2		..	..	5 7	..	..
—	12¼ Wappenham	..	1111		..	..	5 15	..	..
—	16¼ Towcester ......arr	..	1120		..	..	5 22	..	..
—	Towcester ....dep	8 25	1121	1156	..	5 10	5 23	7 52	..
38	Blisworth ....arr	8 36	1130	12 7	..	5 20	5 32	8 2	..
42¼	70 Northampton (C.) arr	8 55	12 0	1250	..	..	5 53	8 20	..
100¾	50 London (Euston).. "	1021	3L44	3J39	..	..	7J45	10J57	..

Miles from Blisworth	Week Days only	a.m	a.m	a.m	a.m	p.m	p.m
	50 London (Euston)..dep	6 40	..	..	12J20	4K35	..
	70 Northampton (C.). "	8 25	9 0	12 17	2 32	6 14	6 14
	Blisworth ....dep	8 55	9 16	12 45	4 0	6 30	6 50
4	Towcester ....arr	9 4	9 26	12 54	4 10	6 42	6 59
—	Towcester ....dep	..	9 27	Sats. only	Except Sats.	6 43	..
8	Wappenham	..	9 36			6 54	..
11¾	Helmdon	..	9 45			7 4	..
16½	Farthinghoe	..	9 57			7 18	..
20½	Banbury D ....arr	..	10 5			7 25	..
—	Towcester ....dep	9 10	..	12 55	4 15	..	7 0
8¼	Blakesley ....[grave	9 18	..	1 4	4 23	..	7 8
11¼	Morton Pinkney, for Sul-	9 26	..	1 11	4 30	..	7 15
15½	Byfield A	9 38	..	1 20	4 39	..	7 27
22	Fenny Compton	9 51	..	1 32	..	..	7 39
28½	Kineton	10 6	..	1 46	..	..	7 51
32½	Ettington	10 15	..	1 55	..	..	7 59
38	Stratford-on-Avon arr	10 26	..	2 6	..	..	8 8

A Station 2 miles from Woodford Halse Station (E.R.) D Merton Street J Via Northampton
K Via Northampton; dep. 3 5 p.m on Sats. L Via Northampton. Arr. 3 17 p.m. on Saturdays

Section 1.

OLNEY

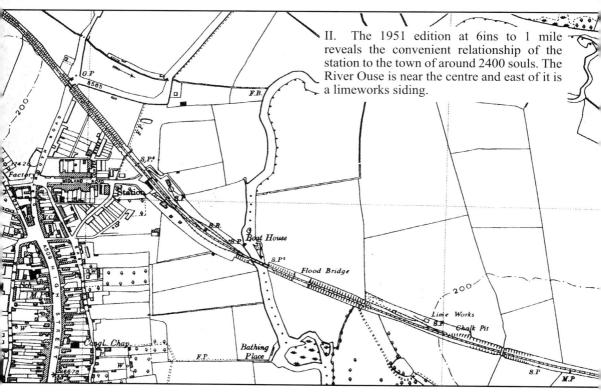

II. The 1951 edition at 6ins to 1 mile reveals the convenient relationship of the station to the town of around 2400 souls. The River Ouse is near the centre and east of it is a limeworks siding.

1. A view towards Bedford on 27th March 1954 features a train being propelled towards Northampton. The water tank on the left would have been supplied with water from the nearby river. (H.C.Casserley)

2. The Northampton service on 13th December 1958 was provided by the ultimate in economical rail transport. The diesel rail bus is no. M79972; these vehicles were withdrawn from the branch in November 1959 to be replaced by two-car DMUs. (G.Adams/M.J.Stretton coll.)

Other photographs of this station can be seen in the *Bedford to Wellingborough* album.

3. Much of the freight on the line was destined for the Towcester route. Ex-MR 0-6-0 no. 43474 is about to start the demanding three-mile climb to Ravenstone Wood Junction, the gradient being severe at 1 in 70 to 80. (Milepost 92½)

4.   The 11.40am Bedford Midland Road to Northampton Castle was propelled by 2-6-2T no. 84005 on 3rd March 1962. This was the last day of passenger service on the route. The goods yard closed on 6th January 1964 and the route between Piddington and Bedford closed totally at that time. (J.Langford)

5.   This is the tank seen in picture no. 1 and it provided shelter for engines of the S&MJR. This company had running powers over the MR to Olney only and thus its locos had to be turned here. (J.Langford)

WEST OF OLNEY

6.   Ravenstone Junction is seen from the signal box, which was in use from 29th June 1891 until 29th June 1958, when the line to Towcester (left) closed. There had been a siding on the right into an Army ammunition store during World War II. (W.A.Camwell/SLS coll.)

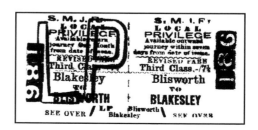

SALCEY FOREST

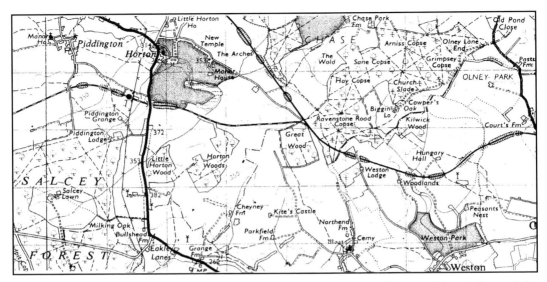

III. The position of the station has been added to the 1954 1ins to 1 mile map. Olney is beyond the right border and Piddington station is above the top one.

7. The provision of a substantial passenger station was an error of judgement as the service lasted less than four months, the dates being given earlier. Local goods traffic was also poor; there had been one siding beyond the platform until 1st July 1908. This view is towards Olney in about 1930. (Stations UK)

8. An inspection train was recorded at the decaying platform in 1950. There had been a signal box behind the camera until 30th September 1912. (R.M.Casserley coll.)

IV. Spare columns were optimistically provided in the timetable in 1892.

TOWCESTER AND OLNEY.

	a. m.	p.m.	p.m.	a.m.	p.m.	p.m.	p.m.		a. m.	a.m.	p. m.	p.m.	p.m.	p.m.	
Towcester..........d	0 26	12 45	6 5	8 10	...	...	...	Olney..............d	8 41	11 51	2 0	6 51	...	...	...
Stoke Bruern........	9 32	12 52	6 13	8 17	...	...	...	Salcey Forest..........	8 51	12 4	2 13	7 4	...	...	...
Salcey Forest..........	9 44	1 4	6 25	8 29	...	...	...	Stoke Bruern..........	9 6	12 16	2 25	7 16	...	...	...
Olney..............a	9 55	1 17	6 40	8 42	...	...	...	Towcester...........a	9 13	12 23	2 32	7 23	...	...	...

ROADE JUNCTION

9.   There was a curve from west to north, south of Roade station, to link the S&MJR with the LNWR. It was open from 13th April 1891 until mid-1917. The southern part was retained as a siding and is seen in July 1951. (R.S.Carpenter coll.)

**Roade station is illustrated in pictures 52-57
in our *Bletchley to Rugby* album.**

10.   This area is in the background of the previous picture and features the former LNWR quadruple track with a down train on it. (R.S.Carpenter coll.)

STOKE BRUERN

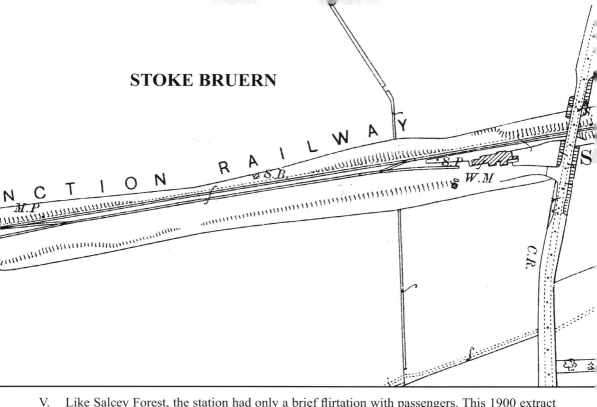

V.   Like Salcey Forest, the station had only a brief flirtation with passengers. This 1900 extract shows the signal box, which lasted in use until 30th September 1912. Thereafter, the block section was an amazing 10½ miles long.

11.   A single wagon stands near the weighing machine (W.M. on the map) on 19th April 1947 and much of the long siding can be seen beyond it. The locality had for long received its domestic coal by canal barge. (W.A.Camwell/SLS coll.)

12.   This photograph is from 4th May 1963, when condemned wagons were stored on the disused line, which had closed in June 1958. Although shown on the map, the crossover at the west end of the siding had been removed in 1912. (J.Langford)

VI.   One mile to the west was Easton Neston siding, which was used by the Towcester Mineral & Brick Co. Ltd in 1909-18, and in a further mile was Towcester Ironstone siding, which was in use in 1919-34. The works and quarries had originally been served from the Blisworth-Towcester route, the fences are shown, far left. The 1905 map is at 6ins to 1 mile.

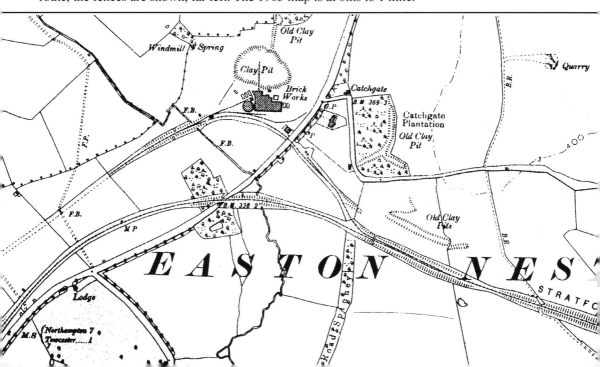

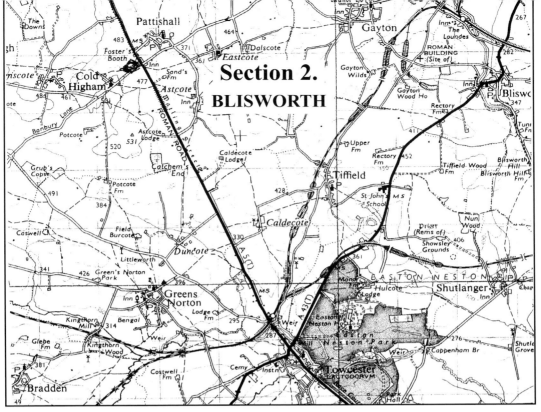

VII. The 1949 edition at 1ins to 1 mile has Blisworth station top right and Towcester at the bottom. Between them is Tiffield, which had a platform until 1871.

13. An eastward panorama from 1930 includes the engine shed and the 42ft turntable provided by the Northampton & Banbury Junction Railway. The shed closed on 10th August 1929. Another turntable was available on the north side of the main line; the near one lasted until 1955. (R.M.Casserley coll.)

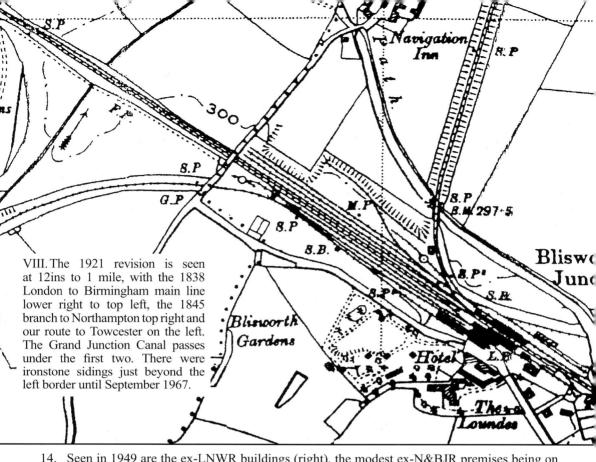

VIII. The 1921 revision is seen at 12ins to 1 mile, with the 1838 London to Birmingham main line lower right to top left, the 1845 branch to Northampton top right and our route to Towcester on the left. The Grand Junction Canal passes under the first two. There were ironstone sidings just beyond the left border until September 1967.

14. Seen in 1949 are the ex-LNWR buildings (right), the modest ex-N&BJR premises being on the left, with coaches standing at its platform. Beyond them is the platform canopy, which was removed in the mid-1950s. (R.M.Casserley coll.)

15. The 12.45pm departure for Stratford waits behind 0-6-0 no. 43568 on 15th March 1952. The tank supplied water to the locomotives via a hydrant and a hose. (H.C.Casserley)

16. Recorded on 5th April 1952 is no. 44567 with the same train. Only the south side of the platform was used for passenger trains after 5th July 1942. Even before this, trains had to reverse out after arrival, for locomotives to run round the coaches. The cattle dock had been on the right. (R.M.Casserley)

17. This signal box was in use from about 1920 until 31st October 1955 and was named BLISWORTH S.M.J. The photograph is from 24th August 1964, when electrification of the main line was in progress. The exchange sidings are to the right of the box and new platform canopies for van traffic can be seen, in white asbestos. (J.C.Gillham)

Other views of this station can be seen in pictures 89 to 93 in _Bletchley to Rugby._

Section 3.
BANBURY
MERTON STREET

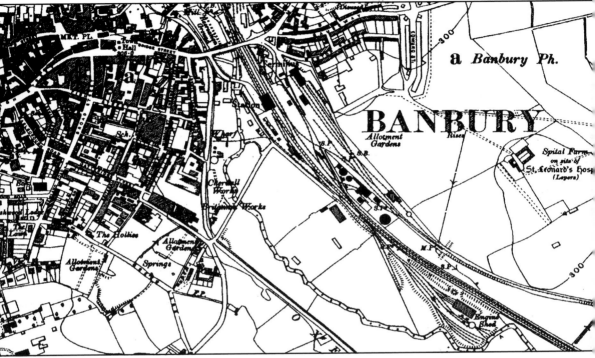

IX. The 1938 map at 6ins to 1 mile has the LMS route to Towcester and Buckingham on the right, above the GWR main line between Oxford and Leamington Spa, which opened from the former in 1850 and to the latter in 1852. There was no connection for through running, only wagon transfer. There had been a massive munitions factory during and after World War I, 1½ miles from the town, with sidings from the LNWR.

18. The approach to the terminus was recorded in 1933, the three-road engine shed being on the left. It could house eight locomotives and was demolished in 1934. The gasworks had sidings from both the LMS and GWR; it closed in 1958. (Mowat coll./Brunel University)

19. There were through coaches from here to Euston via Buckingham and Bletchley between 1901 and 1916. The goods yard was in use until 6th June 1966. No. 42669 is about to leave for Bletchley at 3.42pm on 15th March 1952. The suffix Merton Street had been applied by the LNWR. (H.C.Casserley)

20. The roof covering was removed in stages, but not the framework, which was painted white, along with most items within sight. Blisworth trains had usually used the platform on the right. No. 42669 had arrived at 9.13am with the 8.0 from Bletchley; it is resting prior to returning at 1.40pm on 8th April 1953. (R.M.Casserley)

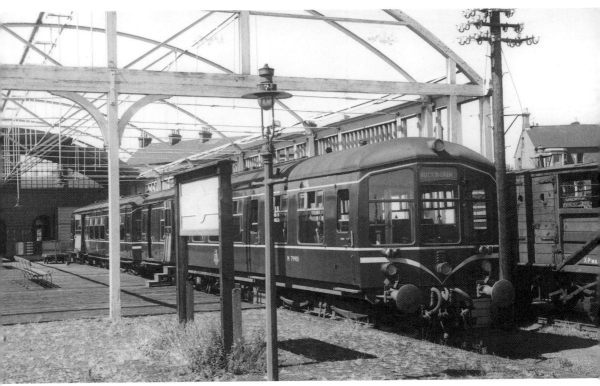

21. Services to Brackley and Buckingham were withdrawn on 2nd January 1961. This train to Buckingham on 4th July 1959 was formed of two Derby Lightweight railcars. One sufficed except on Thursdays (Banbury Market Day) and Saturdays; this was the latter. (J.Langford)

Other albums featuring Banbury include
Banbury to Birmingham, Didcot to Banbury,
Oxford to Bletchley **and** *Princes Risborough to Banbury.*

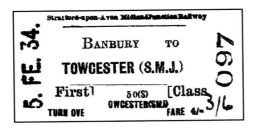

FARTHINGHOE

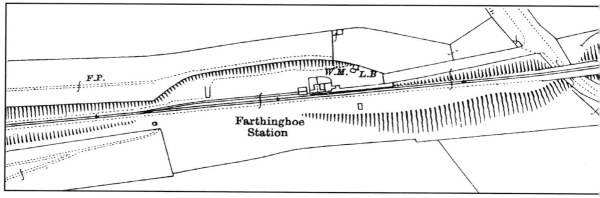

X. A passenger service was provided from October 1851 until 3rd November 1952. The single siding is shown on the 1922 survey.

22. The station building was of timber construction, but the house was of brick. They are seen in 1933. The siding once handled traffic for RAF Hinton-in-the-Hedges and the yard was in use until the Buckingham route closed completely on 2nd December 1963. The buildings were subsequently destroyed. (R.M.Casserley coll.)

EAST OF FARTHINGHOE

23.   At Cockley Brake Junction, the 1872 Towcester line diverged left from the 1850 Buckingham route. Both were single lines, but there was double track in front of the signal box. The photograph is from about 1932. (R.S.Carpenter coll.)

24.   The signal box was in use from 1922 until 12th July 1953 and is seen from a train bound for Bletchley on 18th March 1955, after the levers had been removed. (R.M.Casserley)

HELMDON VILLAGE

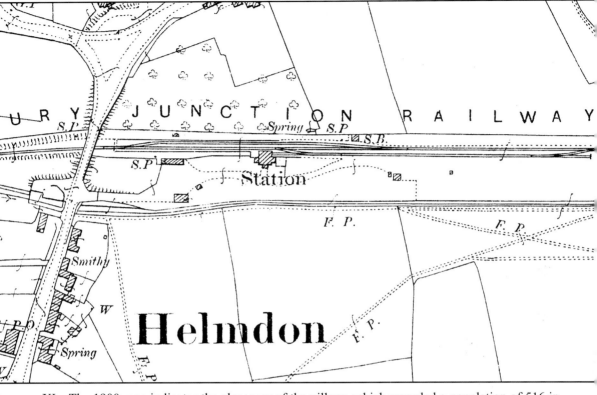

XI. The 1900 map indicates the closeness of the village, which recorded a population of 516 in the following year. The suffix "Village" was added on 1st July 1950, as there was a station of the same name on the ex-GCR route nearby.

25. The red bricks of the goods shed contrasted with the mixed colours of the main building. A feature of many of the dwellings in the attractive village was yellow limestone. This eastward view is from about 1930. Passenger service ceased on 2nd July 1951. (R.S.Carpenter coll.)

26. Goods traffic was withdrawn on 29th October 1951, but the route was usable until 12th July 1953. The photograph is from 1954. The shed contained a 30cwt crane. (Stations UK)

27. The delightful architectural details had been neglected by the time the photographer arrived on 18th June 1958. There had been a signal box here from 1895 until 1901. (R.M.Casserley)

WAPPENHAM

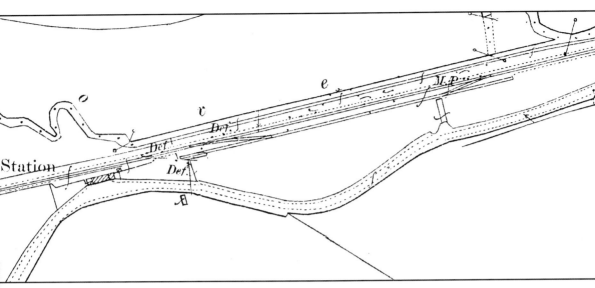

XII. The 1900 survey reveals how the River Tove had to be straightened to run parallel to the railway. The population was only 383 in 1901. The siding was of value to RAF Silverstone during World War II.

28. The structure was to the same design as that at Helmdon and the dates were identical. Class 4F 0-6-0 no. 44204 hauls a Banbury-Blisworth train on the last day of passenger service, 30th June 1951. (R.S.Carpenter coll.)

29.   An eastward view in 1954 includes a twin-arch road bridge optimistically built in anticipation of a double track main line between the Midlands and South Wales. (Stations UK)

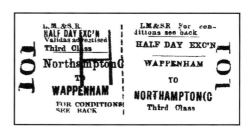

Section 4.

BROOM JUNCTION

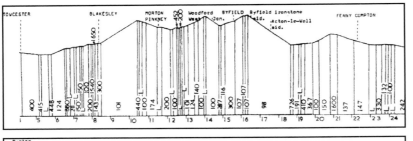

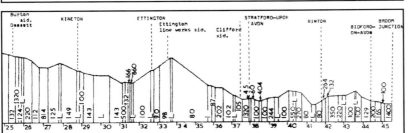

XIII. The Barnt Green to Ashchurch line is from top right to lower left on this 1922 extract, while the Towcester route is at the bottom. An east-south spur (south of this map) was opened on 28th September 1942 to make a triangular junction, which would facilitate the passage of iron ore trains from the Midlands to South Wales.

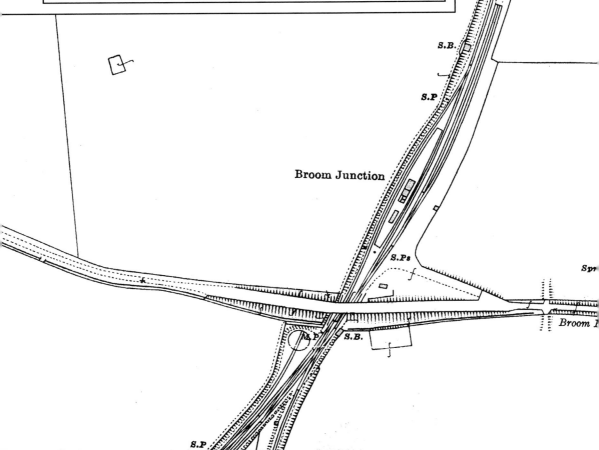

30. A 1930 southward panorama has our route on the left and the line to Evesham in the centre. The turntable was 40ft 10ins in length and was in use until 1957. (C.Gilbert/R.S.Carpenter coll.)

Other views of Broom Junction appear in
Cheltenham to Redditch, **pictures 16 to 73.**

31. The map shows two signal boxes (North and South), but these were replaced by the one shown here on 6th May 1934. It was known as Junction until 17th May 1942, when it became North and two others opened. The photo is from 22nd April 1962. (J.Langford)

32.   It is August 1962 and all three signal boxes had been closed on 5th July of that year. Passenger trains ran between Evesham and Redditch until 1st October of that year. The coach body had been added to give more accommodation. Local freight traffic ceased on 13th June 1960; the wagons seen are stored out of use. (W.A.Camwell/SLS coll.)

33.   A sectional concrete shed was provided as more durable space. The photograph is from 25th August 1964. Initially, the station was just a junction, but locals were allowed to use it from 1st November 1880. (J.C.Gillham)

34.   This is Broom East box on 22nd April 1962, with the 1942 curve on the left. It had a 14-lever frame, while North had 35 levers and West had 15. (J.Langford)

FIRST CLASS
Issued by the E. & W. J. R. Co.'s subject to the Co.'s regulations and to the conditions in the Time Tables of the respective Companies over whose Lines this Ticket is available.

Stratford-on-Avon to
BROOM

BROOM

273

East & West Junction & Stratford-on-Avon, Towcester & Midland Junction Railways. — This Ticket is issue subject to the Regulations and Conditions stated in the Time Tables & Bills of the respective Companies over whose Lines this ticket is available.

Third Class Parly   Third Class Parly
Stratford-on-Avon to
BROOM
FARE 7¼d.   FARE 7¼d.

S.on Avon-Broom   S.on Avon-Broom

975   975

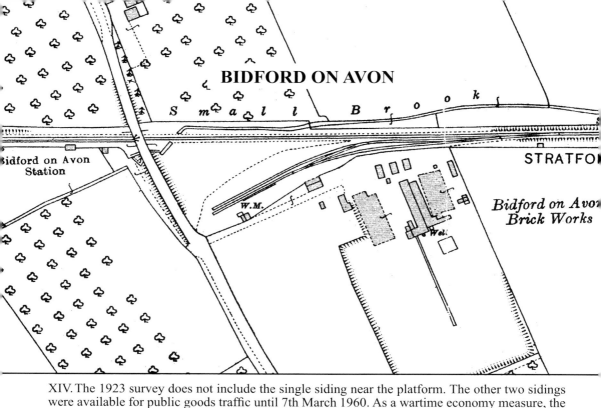

BIDFORD ON AVON

S m a l l   B r o o k

Bidford on Avon
Station

STRATFO

W. M.

Bidford on Avon
Brick Works

Wel

XIV. The 1923 survey does not include the single siding near the platform. The other two sidings were available for public goods traffic until 7th March 1960. As a wartime economy measure, the station was closed from 19th February 1917 until 1st January 1919. It closed temporarily again on 16th June 1947, but never reopened. There were signals until 1931.

35.   The siding and two fruit baskets can be seen through the fence in this eastward view from about 1924. The second arch in the road bridge was never used for track; instead it was converted for staff use and a ticket office. The station opened two years after the line, in 1881.
(Stations UK)

36. The two sidings of the eastern goods yard are seen in about 1949, as an LMS mobile crane waits to unload the pipes behind it. On the right is the weigh house. (J.Moss/R.S.Carpenter coll.)

37. A special called in 1955 and generated probably the biggest crowd ever at this location. There had been a van body in use as a parcels shed near the trees. The suffix had been added on 1st July 1909. (Stations UK)

BINTON

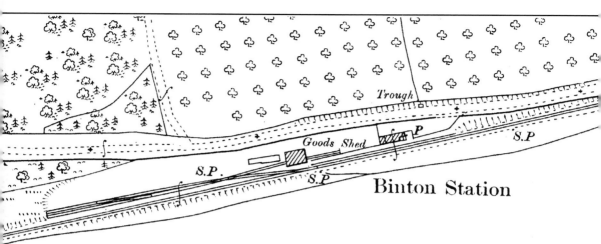

XV. The map is from 1901, but the other dates shown under the Bidford map also apply here. Conversely this station opened with the line. There were signals here until 1922.

38. We look west in June 1934 when there could be as many as four passenger trains per day each way to disturb the peace of this tranquil location. There were 228 village residents recorded in 1901. (Mowat coll./Brunel University)

39. This photograph was taken at the same time as no. 36 and includes the same commodities. Two ground frames controlled access to the siding, but the nearest connection was removed in January 1956.
(J.Moss/
R.S.Carpenter coll.)

40. The road frontage was recorded in May 1951, four years after the last passenger had passed through the door. The unroofed part contained facilities for gentlemen.
(R.S.Carpenter coll.)

41. Plums had been a notable traffic loaded here in quantity for many years. The inclined fencing pales were a feature to be found widely on MR routes. The photograph is from April 1959.
(R.M.Casserley)

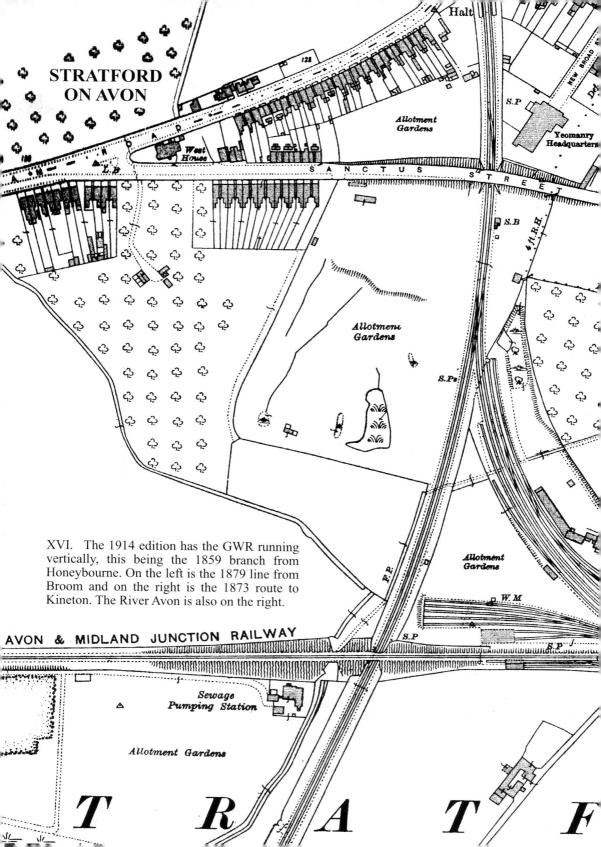

**STRATFORD
ON AVON**

Halt

*Allotment
Gardens*

West
House

Yeomanry
Headquarters

S A N C T U S   S T R E E

*Allotment
Gardens*

XVI. The 1914 edition has the GWR running vertically, this being the 1859 branch from Honeybourne. On the left is the 1879 line from Broom and on the right is the 1873 route to Kineton. The River Avon is also on the right.

*Allotment
Gardens*

W. M

AVON & MIDLAND JUNCTION RAILWAY

*Sewage
Pumping Station*

Allotment Gardens

T   R   A   T   F

42.   An 1897 record includes the early low-level platforms and four-wheeled coaches. The loco is an E&WJR 2-4-0T and is air braked. (Ted Hancock Books)

43.   The 0-6-0 was the most successful type of locomotive on the route. This is S&MJR no. 15 and is seen in 1919. It was built by Beyer Peacock in 1904 and ran until 1924. (P.Q.Treloar coll.)

44.   An eastward panorama from about 1932 emphasises the close relationship of the loco sheds to the station. The turntable pit is on the right; it was 51ft 8ins in diameter. (R.S.Carpenter coll.)

Other pictures of Stratford appear in
Stratford upon Avon to Cheltenham
and *Stratford upon Avon to Birmingham*.

---

45.   This experimental vehicle, called the Ro-Railer, was built by Karrier Motors and fitted with a Cravens body. Its details can be seen in pictures 49-51 in *Branch Line to Hemel Hempstead* during trials. The road wheels were on eccentrics fitted to extensions to the rail wheel axles. The changeover was done on boarded track behind the signal box and it took 2½ to 5 minutes. The road wheels are here locked to the chassis. (LMS)

46. Another photograph from the launch in April 1932 and this shows luggage being loaded in two ways. It is outside the LMSR's Welcombe Hotel, one mile north of the town. Blisworth was the other end of the journey, which was undertaken at up to 50mph. Petrol consumption was 8mpg on the road and 16 on the rails. The rail wheels can be seen inside the others. There was seating for 22 and the service lasted about three months. (LMS)

47. The north elevation was photographed in the early 1930s, together with the former E&WJR signal box (right), which had ceased to function as such in 1919. In the foreground is the siding leading to Lucy & Nephew's corn mill. From October 1943, it also served a Government grain silo. (LMS)

48. The awning on the up side was built in 1919 and was photographed in 1934. The building included a refreshment room. The left signal was for the engine shed, the centre one for Broom and the right one for the GWR connection. The goods yard closed on 11th November 1963. (Mowat coll./Brunel University)

49. The lamp room is the building to the left of 0-6-0 no. 43693, which has just arrived from Blisworth on 10th April 1949. To the left of the water column is a fire devil to prevent it freezing. (R.S.Carpenter coll.)

50. The new connection to the Western Region is on the left. Also seen is the crane, which was of 6-ton capacity. The early signal box and rodding tunnel are on the right and are seen in April 1956. The other box had 30 levers and closed on 12th June 1960, when the east-south double track connection came into use. The east-north single line lasted until 1st March 1965; it had been double until 1958. (R.M.Casserley)

51. The Royal Train waits to depart east behind 4-6-0 no. 44919 in 1964. Her Majesty spent the night in Clifford Sidings. The signals were controlled at that time by Evesham Road Crossing Box. The route east to Kineton also closed completely on 1st March 1965, along with the new curve. (Milepost 92½)

Engine Shed

52. The first engine on the E&WJR was this 1866 Manning Wardle 0-6-0ST and it remained until 1910. It is seen in May 1904 with a GCR coach. It was sold to the Shropshire & Montgomeryshire Railway and moved to the West Sussex Railway in 1924. By then named *Morous*, it was scrapped in about 1935. (K.Nunn/P.Q.Treloar coll.)

53. The company bought six new engines from Beyer Peacock in 1873, but owing to its severe financial problems, all were sold in 1875. To maintain its goods service, the firm purchased this double Fairlie from the Yorkshire Engine Company in 1876. It had been built for Mexico and was probably a bargain. A single Fairlie came too; both went in 1877. (A.Dudman coll.)

54. The shed was opened in 1876, extended in 1908 and rebuilt in 1935. The locomotive details are in captions 43 and 52. (P.Q.Treloar coll.)

55. The Edge Hill Railway's two ex-London Brighton & South Coast Railway "Terrier" 0-6-0s were unusual visitors to the shed in about 1922. They are air braked. (R.S.Carpenter coll.)

56. Under the lifting gantry in 1931 is LMS 0-6-0 no. 3695. At the east end of the sheds until 1928 was a steam driven generator supplying electricity to the station and shed lights. (R.M.Casserley)

57. Here is the 1935 shed complex on 29th April 1956. There were no engines allocated here after February 1953, but they were serviced until 22nd July 1957. The coal stage shelter is in the foreground. (R.M.Casserley)

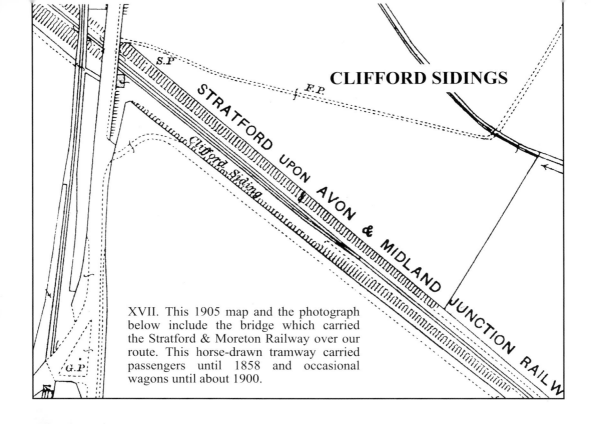

CLIFFORD SIDINGS

S.P

F.P

STRATFORD UPON AVON & MIDLAND JUNCTION RAILW

Clifford Siding

G.P

XVII. This 1905 map and the photograph below include the bridge which carried the Stratford & Moreton Railway over our route. This horse-drawn tramway carried passengers until 1858 and occasional wagons until about 1900.

58. This and the next picture are from September 1921. The southern section of the tramway became part of the Shipston-on-Stour branch, which features in pictures 107-120 in *Oxford to Moreton-in-Marsh*. This also contains a map of the Stratford upon Avon terminus, which was on the north side of the river. Lower right is the buffer stop of Clifford Siding. (R.S.Carpenter coll.)

59. Looking east from the bridge, we see the single siding, which was replaced by two, further south, in 1942, when a signal box was built in the middle distance. The sidings also served Atherstone Airfield during World War II. (R.S.Carpenter coll.)

60.   The box had 20 levers and was in use from 27th September 1942 until 1st March 1965, double track to Stratford being available in that period. On the right is the long refuge siding; the others were in use for public goods traffic until 4th November 1963. Ex-WD 2-8-0 no. 90066 is hauling a train of old rails in about 1962. A village nearby was called Clifford Chambers. (P.Coutanche)

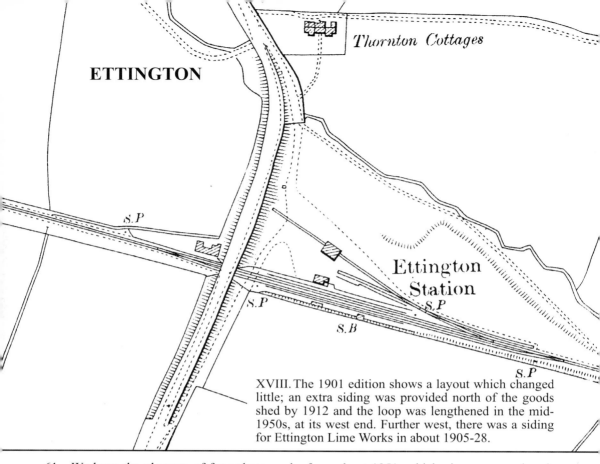

ETTINGTON

Thornton Cottages

S.P

S.P

S.B

S.P

Ettington
Station

S.P

S.P

XVIII. The 1901 edition shows a layout which changed little; an extra siding was provided north of the goods shed by 1912 and the loop was lengthened in the mid-1950s, at its west end. Further west, there was a siding for Ettington Lime Works in about 1905-28.

61. We have the pleasure of four photographs from about 1951, which give a comprehensive overview of all the structures. This includes one of the two barrow crossings, both of which could be used by passengers. The centre one was for staff only. (J.Moss/R.S.Carpenter coll.)

62.   No dwellings are in sight; the village was around one mile distant and it had only 716 residents by 1961. The station served Wellesbourne Airfield, together with Army and prisoner of war camps during World War II. (J.Moss/R.S.Carpenter coll.)

63.   This view reveals that there was no entrance on the approach road side of the building. There was limited local goods traffic, but an unexpected one of note passing through regularly was bananas from Avonmouth to London. (J.Moss/R.S.Carpenter coll.)

64.   The chalked 23 was for the benefit of the pointsmen in hump marshalling yards. The building on the right is adjacent to the weighbridge and the station house is beyond the cattle pens. The goods yard closed on 11th November 1963. (J.Moss/R.S.Carpenter coll.)

65.   After the platforms were removed, new facilities were provided for the signalman to exchange the single line staffs. The box had 13 levers and was in use until line closure on 1st March 1965. It was photographed in May 1962. (P.Kingston)

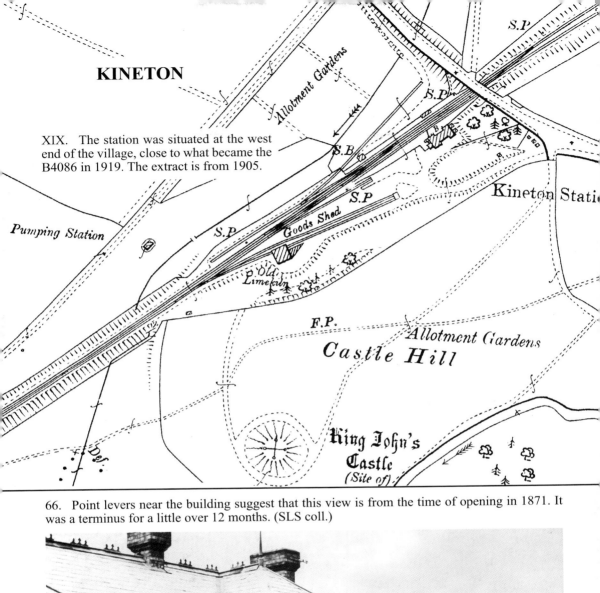

KINETON

XIX. The station was situated at the west end of the village, close to what became the B4086 in 1919. The extract is from 1905.

Allotment Gardens

S.P.

S.P.

S.B.

Kineton Station

Pumping Station

S.P.

S.P.

Goods Shed

Old Limekiln

F.P.

Allotment Gardens

Castle Hill

Def.

King John's Castle (Site of)

66. Point levers near the building suggest that this view is from the time of opening in 1871. It was a terminus for a little over 12 months. (SLS coll.)

67. An eastward view in about 1924 includes vans standing beyond the end of the loop and the traditional row of fire buckets conveniently close to the conveniences for refilling. (Stations UK)

68.   A horse box stands on the line to the cattle dock in about 1950. The up sidings are included in this view, which also contains the LMS "Hawkseye" nameboard. (J.Moss/R.S.Carpenter)

69.   The village population rose from 1008 in 1901 to 1349 in 1961. This picture is from October 1950, only two years before the last passenger would walk along this road. (R.S.Carpenter coll.)

70. This is the last day of regular passenger service, 5th April 1952, and 0-6-0 no. 44525 carries a suitable message to station staff. The loop was greatly extended in 1958. (SLS coll.)

➔ 71. The token is passed across the footplate of 0-6-0 no. 44491 on 19th October 1957 to the crew of 0-6-0 no. 44266. On the right is the parcels shed and the lamp room. (P.Q. Treloar)

➔ 72. The cattle pens are evident as Railway Enthusiasts Club members record the scene and ex-GWR "Dukedog" 4-4-0 no. 9015 on 24th April 1955. The signal box had a 24-lever frame and functioned to the end of through traffic. (H. Ballantyne)

Stratford-upon-Avon & Midland Junction Railway.
This ticket is issued subject to the Regulations and conditions stated in the Company's Time Tables & Bills.
Third Class   Third Class
Available on day of issue only
KINETON to
BYFIELD
FARE   FARE
Kineton-Byfield   Kineton-Byfield
1308   1308

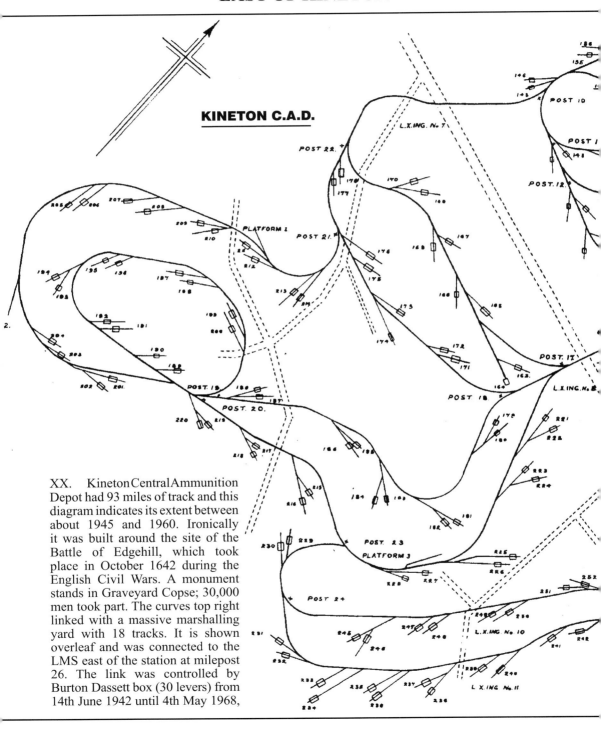

KINETON C.A.D.

XX. Kineton Central Ammunition Depot had 93 miles of track and this diagram indicates its extent between about 1945 and 1960. Ironically it was built around the site of the Battle of Edgehill, which took place in October 1642 during the English Civil Wars. A monument stands in Graveyard Copse; 30,000 men took part. The curves top right linked with a massive marshalling yard with 18 tracks. It is shown overleaf and was connected to the LMS east of the station at milepost 26. The link was controlled by Burton Dassett box (30 levers) from 14th June 1942 until 4th May 1968,

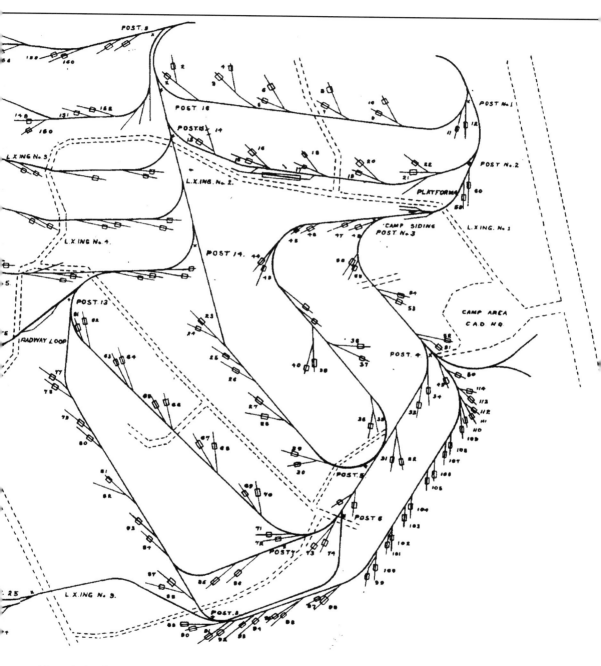

although the line westward had closed on 1st March 1965. The word POST refers to block posts indicating operational boundaries; telephone permission was required to enter the next one. The connection was three miles from Kineton station.

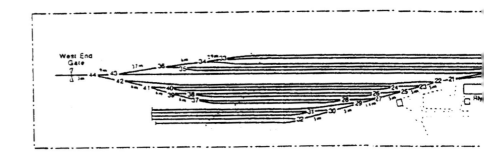

DEFENCE RAIL KINETON

XXI. The 1995 diagram shows a track mileage of 23, but the distances are indicated in metres. The top diagram is of the marshalling yard and the connection to the main line is top right. This was worked by MOD locomotives until 2001 and EWS subsequently. By 2008, the carriage & wagon shed had become a tool store and the railcar shed the loco shed. The loco shed was used for training purposes.

Key

14	Markerpost
LC 6	Level crossing
⚐	Gate

'D' Br

'E' Branch

'D' Bran

LC 13
LC 6
LC 27
LC 26
LC 25
LC 5
13

Plate Layers
Siding
LC 15
LC 14

'F' Branch
LC 23

Edge Hill Site

RRT 4
RRT 5
LC 20
LC 19
LC 21
LC 22
LC 49

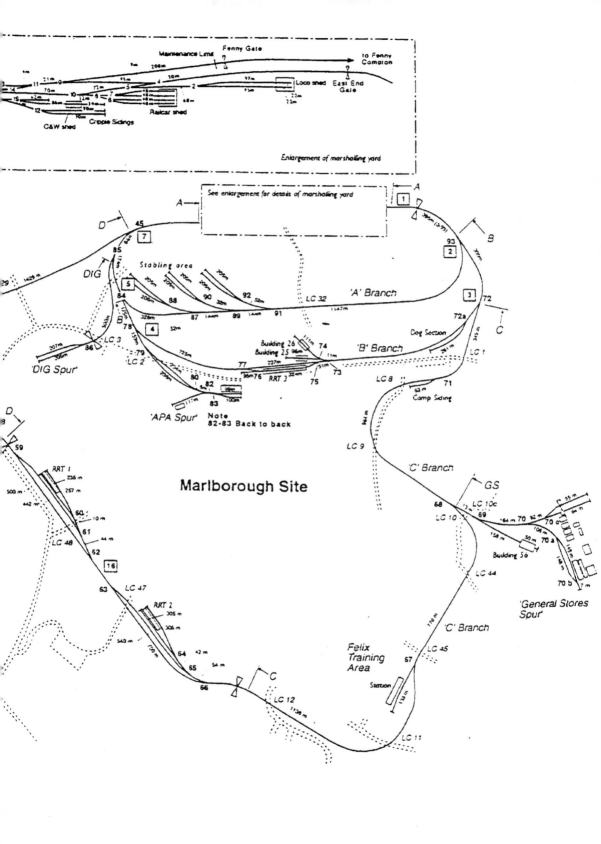

Marlborough Site

73. The marshalling yard is seen from the west in 1992, the year in which an SLS railtour entered the site. The route of the former line from Stratford is top left. (Kineton Railway Archive)

74. Her Majesty Queen Elizabeth II visited the site on 24th March 1988 to open the Edge Hill sub-depot. Recorded that day were Steelmans and Vanguards outside the loco shed. All were built by Thomas Hill in the late 1970s and early 1980s. (Kineton Railway Archive)

75. The replica *Rocket* came from the National Railway Museum on the occasion of the retirement of a senior officer in January 1994. On the left are class 323 DMUs awaiting service with Regional Railways and centre is a platform (plus signals) erected for an open day. The vans would convey ammunition to places such as Caerwent and Marchwood. (Kineton Railway Archive)

76.   This eastward panorama from 24th July 2008 includes the former locomotive shed, together with the railway offices and control room. The engine is Vanguard no. 01546 and it is also seen in the next picture. (V.Mitchell)

77.   Looking west from the control room on the same day, we see retired Virgin Mk. 3 coaches in store. Rental of storage space began in 1992 and coach numbers peaked at over 400 later, while passengers continued to stand in peak hours. (V.Mitchell)

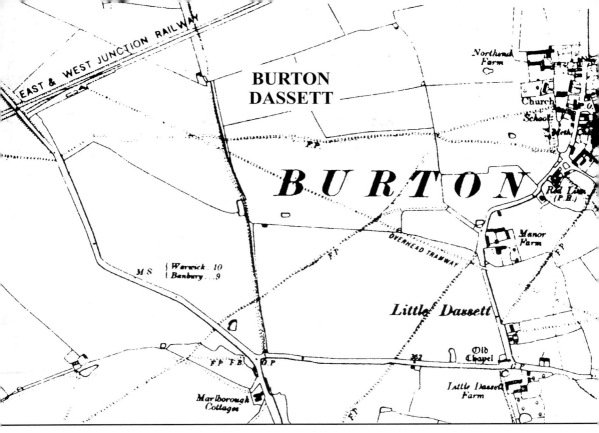

XXII. The 1905 map at 12ins to 1 mile has the sidings top left and part of the village top right. There had been a station on the south side of the line called Warwick Road until 1873. The sidings were brought into use in 1898 for loading ironstone from an aerial ropeway, wrongly shown as TRAMWAY. They conveyed general goods traffic from 1909.

78. The platform was never available for public use and is seen in the early 1920s. The building was used as an office for the goods depot foreman until 27th January 1925. (Dr. J.R.Hollick)

79.   A 1951 photograph features the platform, which was west of the A41 and was known to have been used in 1909-18. It probably also functioned during World War II, but was never publicised. The second track was laid down in 1942 and was about ½ mile in length and was termed a down loop from 1958. (R.M.Casserley coll.)

XXIII. The 1949 survey at 1ins to 1 mile shows a mineral line curving south from the A41 bridge. This had been part of the Edge Hill Light Railway and it was on the land west of it that the extensive Central Ammunition Depot was developed. There is no evidence of it, for security reasons. Edge Hill is at the bottom of the map. There was a platform at Northend (top) until 1877.

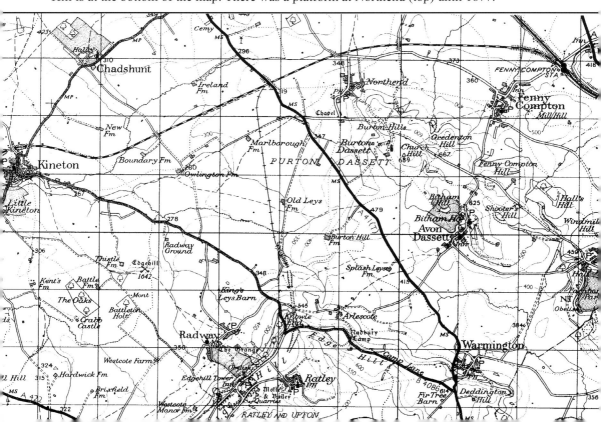

EDGE HILL LIGHT RAILWAY

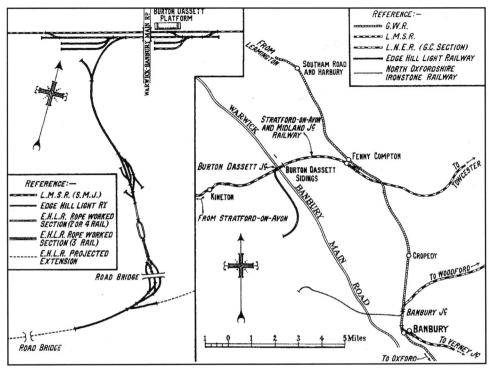

XXIV. The line was promoted by the S&MJR in 1917 to help meet wartime iron demands, but by the time it opened on 22nd January 1922, this did not apply. The railway was never completed and closed on 27th January 1925. (Railway Magazine)

80.　The bridge shown in picture 79 is seen from the other side on 18th October 1930, with the EHLR track curving towards the incline. (R.S.Carpenter coll.)

81.   We are now at the foot of the rope-worked incline, which was at the gradient of 1 in 9. The date is 12th September 1938. The ironstone was of inferior quality and not worth using in the next war. (R.S.Carpenter coll.)

82.   The top of the balance incline is seen later in 1938; a rope is evident on the right. The diagram shows the passing loop. On the left is the brakesman's hut. (R.S.Carpenter coll.)

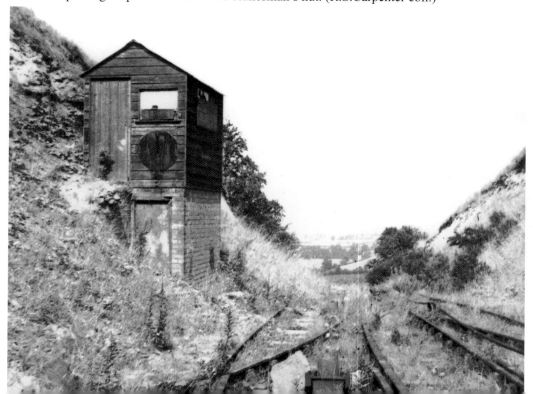

83. Manning Wardle 0-4-0ST *Sankey* worked the upper level, but had no shed. It is seen with a road bridge as shelter on 30th June 1940. (L.W.Perkins/F.A.Wycherley)

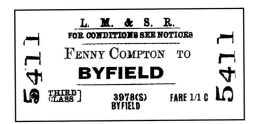

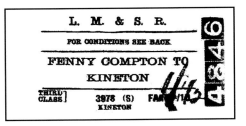

84.　Recorded on the same day is one of the two Terrier 0-6-0Ts used in the exchange sidings. This is EHLR no. 2, formerly LBSCR no. 674 *Shadwell*, with an ex-GER brake van and other remnants. (L.W.Perkins/F.A.Wycherley)

85.　On the right is no. 1, ex-LBSCR no. 673 *Deptford*, on 25th June 1945. Most of the track was lifted in 1942, but the three locos were not cut up until 1946, despite the need for steel in WWII. (A.N.H.Glover/F.A.Wycherley)

FENNY COMPTON WEST

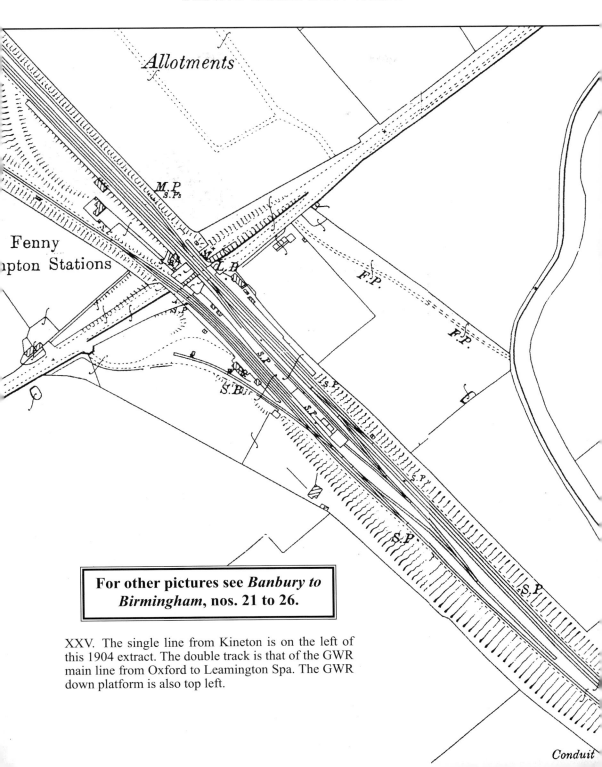

Allotments

Fenny
mpton Stations

For other pictures see *Banbury to Birmingham*, nos. 21 to 26.

XXV. The single line from Kineton is on the left of this 1904 extract. The double track is that of the GWR main line from Oxford to Leamington Spa. The GWR down platform is also top left.

Conduit

86. Bound for Stratford upon Avon in about 1939 is 0-6-0 no. 3529. The wagons to the left of it are on the exchange siding between the LMS and the GWR. It did not allow through running. (Stations UK)

87. The signal box was unusual in that it had two frames: 20 levers for the LMS and 29 for the GWR. They were in use from June 1931 until March 1960. There was a joint stationmaster for much of that period. This March 1952 photograph shows the platform for trains to Towcester, the low underbridge and the level crossing for vehicles too tall to use it. (H.C.Casserley)

88. The former GWR up platform is on the right of this 1952 northward view; both closed on 2nd November 1964. On the left is the small goods yard, which was in use until 4th May 1964. The ex-S&MJR platform in the centre was removed in 1960 to allow direct connections between the two routes.
(H.C.Casserley)

89. A new signal box was opened on 7th March 1960 and was snapped from a passing train on 26th June 2002. It had 77 levers and closed on 1st May 2004, after which time the junction was controlled from Leamington Spa.
(V.Mitchell)

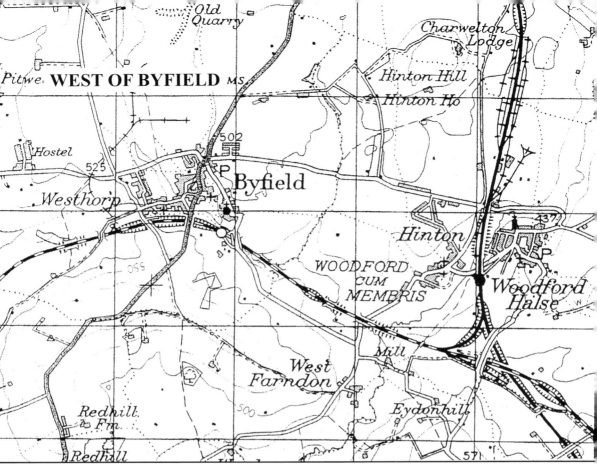

XXVI. The 1953 edition shows a mineral line running north of Byfield. It was opened in May 1915 by the Northamptonshire Ironstone Company and taken over by the Byfield Ironstone Company in November 1928.

90. Traffic at the siding ceased on 15th February 1965, the quarry having been operated by the Staveley Coal & Iron Co. Ltd. since 1941. *No. 3 Avonside* is seen on 24th April 1965. Gradients were up to 1 in 25 and 80 loaded wagons were often sent away each day. (D.A.Johnson)

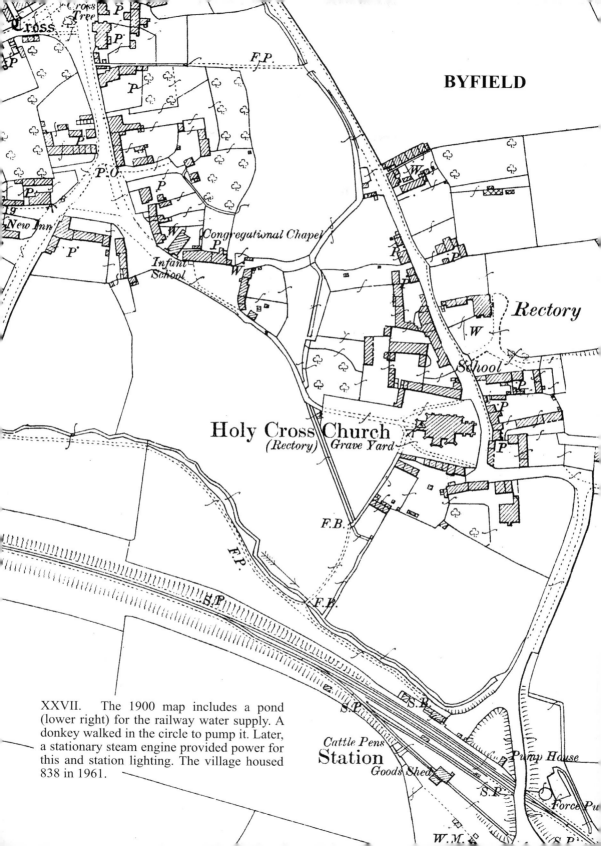

BYFIELD

Cross
Cross Tree

F.P.

P.O.

New Inn

Congregational Chapel

W

Infant School

W

Rectory

W

School

Holy Cross Church
(Rectory) Grave Yard

F.B.

F.P.

S.P.

F.B.

XXVII. The 1900 map includes a pond
(lower right) for the railway water supply. A
donkey walked in the circle to pump it. Later,
a stationary steam engine provided power for
this and station lighting. The village housed
838 in 1961.

S.P.

Cattle Pens
Station

Goods Shed

Pump House

S.P.

Force Pu

W.M.

S.P.

91.   May 1932 and the goods yard appears full; the 30cwt crane is evident. The cattle pens are less clear; these were busy on market days, which were once every two weeks.
(Mowat coll./Brunel University)

92.   Heading the 6.50pm Blisworth to Stratford on 17th May 1951 is 0-6-0 no. 44242 and it is passing the 6.40 Stratford to Blisworth at 7.27. A coach body is almost hidden on the up platform.
(T.J.Edgington)

93.   The SMJR Railtour on 29th April 1956 was worked by 0-6-0 no. 43222. The train had started from Kings Cross at 9.14 and run via Hertford and Bedford. It returned via Broom, Redditch and Birmingham New Street to Euston, all for 24 shillings. (R.M.Casserley)

94.   An eastward view on 16th June 1958 shows the loop to be longer than that on the map. It had been extended in 1919. The seats vanished in 1952, as did the passengers. (H.C.Casserley)

95. This trolley is in the previous picture, as is this crossing. The E&WJR was originally laid with keys inside the rails. (R.M.Casserley)

96. The goods yard was in use until 4th May 1964 and is seen on 31st May 1963. Both lines were signalled for reversible running. The siding near the platform was added around 1898. (B.W.L.Brooksbank)

EAST OF BYFIELD

97. Reference to the map above picture 90 will help to explain the complex junction with the former GCR, which is shown with a solid line. We look east at Woodford West Junction in 1933, with the line curving north to Woodford Halse on the left. This was in use from September 1899 until February 1965. Centre is the single line to Towcester and the sidings on the right had formed a double track connection to the GCR from March 1899 until October 1900. (R.M.Casserley coll.)

98.   Eastbound on 6th May 1963 is 0-6-0 44296 and it is passing over the ex-GCR route between Marylebone and Leicester, this part opening in 1898. (N.Sprinks)

99.   Travelling westwards and passing over the same bridge is ex-MR 0-6-0 no. 43873 on 9th March 1957. The main line was in use until 1966 and is featured in our *Aylesbury to Rugby* album. (N.Sprinks)

100. Looking west from the signal box featured in picture 97, we witness class L1 2-6-4T no. 67789 working a transfer freight to the extensive yards north of Woodford Halse station. In the early 20th century, there had been three passenger trains on this curve on weekdays, but it was reduced to one in the evening by 1951. (N.Sprinks)

L. M. & S. R.
FOR CONDITIONS SEE NOTICES
Byfield to
MORTON PINKNEY
THIRD CLASS]   3979(S)   FARE -/8 C
MORTON PINKNEY
483 X   X 483

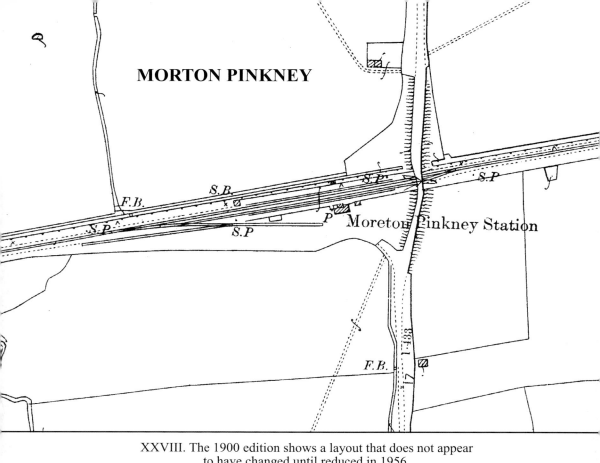

MORTON PINKNEY

F.B.

S.B.

S.P

S.P

S.P

S.P

S.P

P

Moreton Pinkney Station

F.B.

XXVIII. The 1900 edition shows a layout that does not appear
to have changed until reduced in 1956.

101. The facilities were minimal and a coach body had appeared by the time
that this photograph was taken in 1933. (R.M.Casserley coll.)

102. An eastward panorama in 1951 reveals that the loop remained short. On the right is the headshunt for the goods yard, which closed on 7th April 1952. (H.F.Wheeller)

713   713

L. M. & S. R.
FOR CONDITIONS SEE NOTICES
Morton Pinkney to
NORTHAMPTON (CASTLE)
Via BLISWORTH
THIRD CLASS]   3980(S)   FARE 2/11 P
NORTHAMPTON(C.)

4578   4578

L. M. & S. R.
FOR CONDITIONS SEE NOTICES
Morton Pinkney to
TOWCESTER
THIRD CLASS]   3980(S)   FARE 1/4 P
TOWCESTER

103. Photographed in the same year, the box had 12 levers and was usable until 27th May 1956, when the loop was taken out of use. (R.S.Carpenter coll.)

104. By 1959, the site was desolate, but the line continued to be used by freight trains between Woodford West Junction and Blisworth until 7th February 1964. (Stations UK)

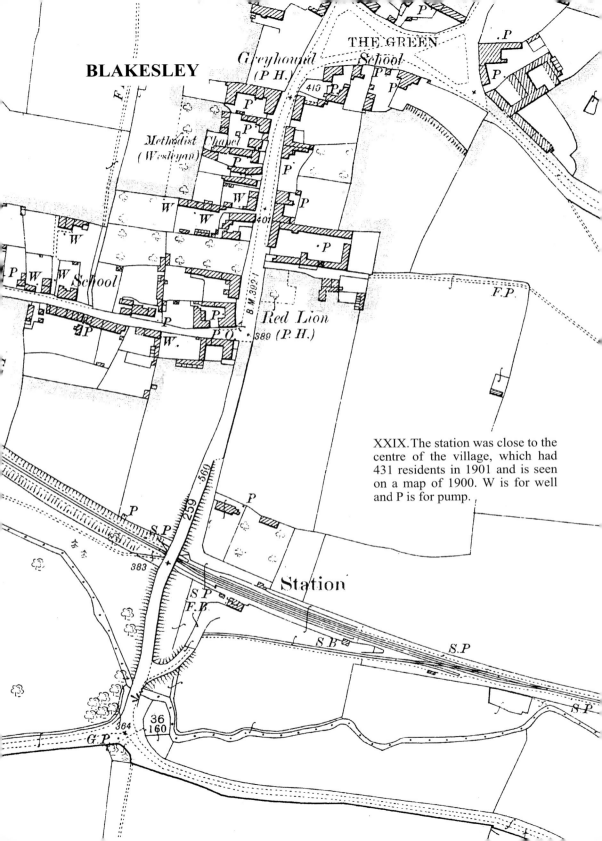

BLAKESLEY

THE GREEN

Greyhound
(P.H.)

School

Methodist Chapel
(Wesleyan)

415

W

W

W

P W W School

P.O.

Red Lion

P

389 (P.H.)

B.M.392·1

401

F.P.

F.P.

560

259

P

S.P.

383

P

Station

S.P.
F.B.

S.B.

S.P.

S.P.

36
160

364

G.P.

XXIX. The station was close to the centre of the village, which had 431 residents in 1901 and is seen on a map of 1900. W is for well and P is for pump.

105. S&MJR 0-6-0 no. 4 was built by Beyer Peacock in 1885 and it is standing with a train of short coaches in the down platform. In the foreground is part of the 15ins gauge line to Blakesley Hall. The rectangles are the sides of tipper wagons used for transport of coal to the house. (P.Q.Treloar coll.)

106. The railway was begun in 1903 by a Yorkshire colliery owner, C.W.Bartholomew, and two Cagney 4-4-0s came from the USA. This 4-4-4 by Greenly housed a two-cylindered petrol engine and was name *Blacolvesley*. The line was lifted in 1940 and the Hall was destroyed in 1957. (P.Q.Treloar coll.)

107. The miniature railway had passed through the left side of this arch. Running to Stratford in about 1951 is 0-6-0 no. 44204. Oil lighting lasted to the end. (H.F.Wheeller)

108. Working the 12.45pm Blisworth to Stratford upon Avon on 15th March 1952 is 0-6-0 no. 43568. Passengers used the crossing in the foreground; the end of their service was imminent. (H.C.Casserley)

109. Six years later and little had changed. Goods yard activity continued until 3rd February 1962. The signal box had 12 levers and seems to have lasted to the end. (R.M.Casserley)

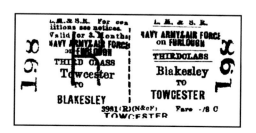

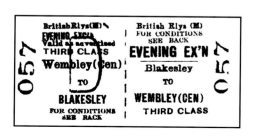

Section 5.
TOWCESTER

XXX. The 1900 survey has the engine shed near the word Hotel and also close to it is the source of much railway revenue, the cattle market. The single siding lower left had three parallel ones added adjacent to it in about 1910. The engine shed was shortened to allow for a bigger cattle dock in 1897. A 42ft turntable was built above the initials GP (Guide Post) in 1908; it remained into the 1940s. Watling Street was of Roman origin and became the A5 in 1919. The map shows two signal boxes; these were replaced by the one illustrated, in June 1910.

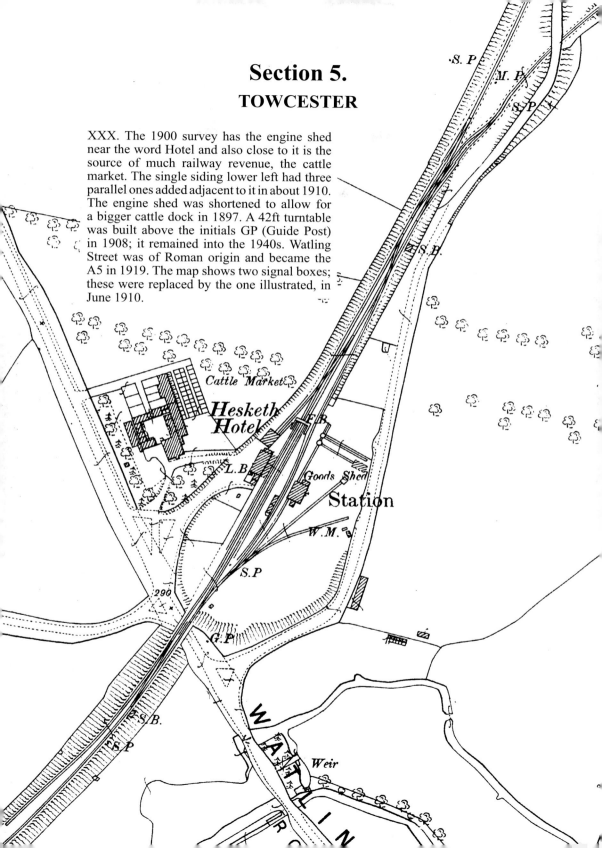

110. A mixed train was recorded in about 1930, with three coaches at the front bound for Blisworth. The third platform (right) was not available for passenger use until 1910. (Stations UK)

111. The signalling at the north end of the site is seen in about 1932, with the freight line to Olney curving to the right. The long siding was a headshunt. (R.S.Carpenter coll.)

112. The trackwork at the north end was recorded in the same era, using an indifferent camera - some would blame the publisher! Each point required two rods, one for locking. (R.S.Carpenter coll.)

113. The engine shed closed in 1929 and Blisworth's was moved here in 1930, but just to act as a store. No. 3551 was working a train to Banbury on 28th March 1932. It was Easter Monday and the Grafton Hunt Steeplechases were being held, thus around 8000 passengers could be expected here that day. (Dr. I.C.Allen/M.J.Stretton coll.)

← 114.   The substantial goods shed and office are in the background as 0-6-0 no. 43520 awaits departure in about 1950. Both hawkseye and totem signs are present. (Stations UK)

← 115.   The south of the station is seen in about 1951 from a train bound for Stratford. Trains for Banbury used the right hand track. Two parallel single lines were provided from 13th June 1910 and Greens Norton Junction was then abolished. (H.F. Wheeller)

116. It is 29th June 1951 and 0-6-0 no. 43573 is at the head of the 4.45pm Banbury to Blisworth, almost the last such train. (T.J. Edgington)

117. The centre running line was removed at the end of 1956, the last scheduled passenger train having departed in April 1952. The cattle pen is visible in this panorama from the signal gantry in July 1958, but the waiting room and canopy have gone. (J.Langford)

118. The turntable site is to the left of the nearest signal post and the point for the line to it is still in place. The two running lines merge in the distance in this view from about 1958. (R.S.Carpenter)

119. Local goods traffic and also ironstone movement ceased on 3rd February 1964; the signal box also closed then. It had a 50-lever frame. The SLS Special on 14th May 1960 seems to have been the only occasion on which a DMU visited the route. (G.Adams/M.J.Stretton coll.)

120. The town grew from 2371 in 1901 to only 2743 by 1961. The one-time headquarters of the S&MJR was photographed in 1965, but was of no interest to the local community. It was bulldozed in favour of an industrial estate. (R.M.Casserley)

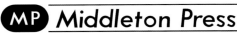
MP Middleton Press

EVOLVING THE ULTIMATE RAIL ENCYCLOPEDIA

Easebourne Lane, Midhurst, West Sussex.
GU29 9AZ   Tel:01730 813169

www.middletonpress.co.uk   email:info@middletonpress.co.uk
A-978 0 906520   B- 978 1 873793   C- 978 1 901706   D-978 1 904474   E - 978 1 906008

OOP Out of print at time of printing - Please check availability   BROCHURE AVAILABLE SHOWING NEW TITLES